HENRI MATISSE

Masterworks from The Museum of Modern Art

HENRI MATISSE

Masterworks from The Museum of Modern Art

An exhibition organized by The Museum of Modern Art
in collaboration with the High Museum of Art

John Elderfield

The Museum of Modern Art, New York

Published on the occasion of the exhibition *Henri Matisse: Masterworks from The Museum of Modern Art*, shown at the High Museum of Art, Atlanta, November 2, 1996–January 19, 1997. The exhibition was organized by The Museum of Modern Art, New York, in collaboration with the High Museum of Art, Atlanta. It was directed by John Elderfield, Chief Curator at Large and Deputy Director for Curatorial Affairs, with Beatrice Kernan, Associate Curator, The Museum of Modern Art. It was coordinated for the High Museum of Art by Carrie Przybilla, Curator of Modern and Contemporary Art, in consultation with Michael E. Shapiro, Deputy Director and Chief Curator.

The High Museum of Art gratefully acknowledges a leadership gift in support of this exhibition from Mr. and Mrs. Holcombe T. Green, Jr.

Additional support has been provided by The Forward Arts Foundation, Inc. of Atlanta, on the occasion of its thirtieth anniversary, and the James Starr Moore Memorial Exhibition Fund.

Produced by the Department of Publications
The Museum of Modern Art, New York
Osa Brown, Director of Publications
Harriet Schoenholz Bee, Managing Editor
Edited by Lucy Adelman O'Brien
Designed by Emily Waters
Production by Amanda W. Freymann and Marc Sapir
Composition by U.S. Lithograph, typographers, New York
Color separation by LS Graphic, Inc., New York/Fotolito Gammacolor, Milan
Printed by LS Graphic, Inc., New York/Grafica Comense, Como

Library of Congress Catalogue Card Number: 96-076144
ISBN: 0-87070-112-6

Published by The Museum of Modern Art
11 West 53 Street, New York, New York 10019

Printed in Italy

COVER: Henri Matisse. *The Red Studio.* 1911. Oil on canvas, 71¼" × 7' 2¼" (181 x 219.1 cm). The Museum of Modern Art, New York. Mrs. Simon Guggenheim Fund (see pp. 66–67)

FRONTISPIECE: Edward Steichen. *Matisse with "La serpentine."* Autumn 1909. Platinum print, 11¹¹⁄₁₆ x 9¼" (29.6 × 23.4 cm). The Museum of Modern Art, New York. Gift of the photographer

*See Photograph Credits at page 149 for additional notices.

CONTENTS

FOREWORD

This publication and the exhibition it accompanies came about through serendipity. At the very moment that The Museum of Modern Art was looking at ways to share its remarkable collection with other museums in the United States, we were approached by the High Museum of Art about our interest in working with them on a series of special exhibitions based on our collection. The result is *Henri Matisse: Masterworks from The Museum of Modern Art,* the first of two exhibitions that we have agreed to develop together.

The Museum of Modern Art's unparalleled collection of the work of Henri Matisse, one of the twentieth century's most celebrated artists, is the result of more than sixty years of assiduous collecting and abiding interest in the artist's work. In its history, the Museum has organized twenty-two Matisse exhibitions of varying size and importance, and has circulated nationally nine Matisse exhibitions, all reflecting its growing collection of the artist's work. This interest in Matisse culminated in The Museum of Modern Art's landmark 1992 exhibition *Henri Matisse: A Retrospective,* organized by John Elderfield. *Henri Matisse* in Atlanta grows out of the Museum's continued commitment to the study of Matisse's prodigious career and is unprecedented in terms of the number and quality of loans from the Museum. The 21 paintings, 16 sculptures, 18 drawings, 10 cutouts, more than 70 prints and illustrated books, 3 liturgical vestments, and 1 stained-glass window that constitute this exhibition represent the core of The Museum of Modern Art's collection of Matisse's work, which has never been lent before to another institution in such concentration. Among the extraordinary objects that make up this exhibition are *The Red Studio,* of 1911, *Piano Lesson,* of 1916, and *The Swimming Pool,* of 1952, each a work of seminal importance that permits us in the context of the exhibition to gain a better understanding of and insight into the artist's achievement, and in so doing to enhance our enjoyment and appreciation of his art.

We are extremely pleased that we are able to share these remarkable works of art with the High Museum of Art. The Museum of Modern Art has long enjoyed a close relationship with both the High Museum and the city of Atlanta. Since 1936, ten exhibitions from The Museum of Modern Art have been seen at the High Museum, including *War Etchings of Otto Dix,* in 1936, *Recent Painting in the USA: The Figure,* in 1963, and *Twentieth-Century Paintings from the Collection of The Museum of Modern Art,* in 1982–83. In addition, The Museum of Modern Art has circulated more than twenty exhibitions to the Atlanta Public Library, Emory University, Georgia State University, and Clark College, among other institutions in Atlanta.

Since its founding in 1929 as an educational institution, The Museum of Modern Art has been committed to the development of a broad understanding of modern art throughout the United States. *Henri Matisse* in Atlanta builds upon the Museum's efforts to fulfill that commitment by sharing its works of art with other institutions. It is our hope that our collaboration with the High Museum of Art on this exhibition and a subsequent one, devoted to the work of Picasso and to be displayed at the High Museum in 1997–98, will lead to a further strengthening of our relationship, and will be of enduring benefit to both museums.

I would like to thank Ned Rifkin, Director, and Michael E. Shapiro, Deputy Director and Chief Curator, both of the High Museum of Art, for their enthusiastic support of this project. At The Museum of Modern Art several individuals played key roles in bringing the exhibition and this publication to fruition. Kirk Varnedoe, Chief Curator, Department of Painting and Sculpture, first proposed that the Museum present a major exhibition of its Matisse collection to the High Museum of Art and supported the initiative from the outset. John Elderfield, Chief Curator at Large and Deputy Director for Curatorial Affairs, undertook the direction of the exhibition for The Museum of Modern Art and wrote the catalogue, bringing to the project his incomparable understanding and knowledge of Matisse. James Snyder, formerly Deputy Director for Planning and Program Support, used his considerable skills in the initial phases of the project to ensure that it would be realized.

The final realization of the exhibition and its accompanying publication crucially depended upon the collaboration and expertise of Beatrice Kernan, Associate Curator and associate director of the 1992 Matisse retrospective. Additional important contributions were made by Richard Palmer, Coordinator of Exhibitions; Elizabeth Addison, Deputy Director for Marketing and Communications; Osa Brown, Director, Department of Publications; as well as by Jennifer Russell, Deputy Director for Exhibition and Collection Support.

Once again we should like to acknowledge the heirs of Henri Matisse and in particular Claude Duthuit, whose commitment is crucial to our endeavor.

Glenn D. Lowry
DIRECTOR, THE MUSEUM OF MODERN ART

PREFACE

As a young person growing up in the New York metropolitan area, I considered myself especially fortunate to have had numerous opportunities to visit The Museum of Modern Art with my family. My mother and father were members and always had Museum of Modern Art exhibition and collection catalogues around our home. Our parents successfully induced me and my siblings to come with them to the Museum with promises of watching Charlie Chaplin movies on Sunday afternoons.

As I matured and my interests in art evolved, I delved into an earnest study of modern art as an undergraduate in college. I found myself returning to the Museum periodically to revisit some of its extensive inventory of modernist icons. Prominent among these was one of my personal favorites, *The Red Studio*, by Henri Matisse. I always found its bold design and radical color astonishing. As I moved further into graduate studies and eventually into teaching the history of modern art at the university level, I became increasingly certain that Matisse was one of the great geniuses of our century.

Today, I write this preface as Director of the High Museum of Art, where it is my pleasure to offer our visitors the great virtues of Matisse's body of work in the full range of mediums of which he was master, including painting, sculpture, drawing, prints and illustrated books, paper cutouts, and stained-glass design. In short, the finest collection of one of the greatest artists of this century comes to Atlanta from an unparalleled museum for the benefit of the residents of the southeastern quadrant of this country. Truly, this is a dream come true for arts educators and parents who would like young people to experience works of art that will resonate in their memories for years to come.

The High is grateful to The Museum of Modern Art, especially to Ronald S. Lauder, Chairman of the Board of Trustees; Agnes Gund, President of the Board of Trustees; Glenn D. Lowry, Director; Kirk Varnedoe, Chief Curator, Department of Painting and Sculpture; and John Elderfield, Chief Curator at Large and Deputy Director for Curatorial Affairs, and a foremost Matisse scholar, for their generosity and cooperation in this unprecedented partnership. In Atlanta, the Board of Directors of the High Museum of Art, led by its Chairman, John Wieland, deserves ample praise for acting quickly and with great conviction to present this exhibition. I also wish to thank my esteemed colleague Michael E. Shapiro, the High Museum's Deputy Director and Chief Curator, for his pivotal role in arranging this important exhibition, as well as Anne Baker, Director of External Affairs, and Rhonda Matheison, Director of Business Affairs, for their support,

encouragement, and good work in realizing this project. I am deeply grateful to Carrie Przybilla, our new Curator of Modern and Contemporary Art, for coordinating the many details involved in the mounting of *Henri Matisse: Masterworks from The Museum of Modern Art.*

Of course, no exhibition of this magnitude would be possible without the critical and timely support of individuals and foundations that represent an institution's most devoted patrons and friends. In the case of this project, the High Museum of Art is fortunate to have received a leadership gift from Nancy and Holcombe T. Green, Jr., collectors, philanthropists, and dedicated volunteers at the Museum. Not only have they stepped forward to support this exhibition, but they have also recently endowed the director's chair at the High, an act of great generosity and vision. For this, as well as for their personal friendship, I wish to extend my most profound gratitude.

There are organizations that stand with you over the years to bring dreams into reality. The Forward Arts Foundation, Inc. of Atlanta, celebrating its thirtieth anniversary in 1997, has always supported the High Museum of Art with revenues generated through sales at their Swan Coach House and through other fund-raising activities. In celebration of this anniversary, the Foundation has brought its extraordinary resources together to assist the High with this important undertaking. The friendship and mutual respect between the Foundation and the Museum is considerable, sharing numerous leaders, patrons, and working members. I know that the High Museum of Art would not be what it is today without the Forward Arts Foundation's great and strong support.

In addition, a founding trustee of the Forward Arts Foundation is Mrs. O. Ray Moore. Thanks to Mrs. Moore and to Ms. Starr Moore, the High enjoys support for its James Starr Moore Memorial Exhibition Fund, which will assist in the presentation of *Henri Matisse: Masterworks from The Museum of Modern Art.* The generosity and thoughtfulness with which the Moore family has championed this institution is a model of philanthropy.

Finally, it is indeed a great honor and privilege for the High Museum of Art to be the exclusive venue of this rare loan of more than one hundred works by Matisse from this exceptional collection. We hope that our visitors will take advantage of this opportunity to become familiar with the many fine works by this outstanding artist.

Ned Rifkin
NANCY AND HOLCOMBE T. GREEN, JR. DIRECTOR
HIGH MUSEUM OF ART

15/30
Henri Matisse

Henri Matisse Etching. *[1900–03]. Drypoint, printed in black: composition 5 5/16 × 7 7/8" (15.1 × 20.1 cm); sheet 13 × 20 1/16" (32.9 × 51 cm).*
The Museum of Modern Art, New York. Gift of Mrs. Bertram Smith

INTRODUCTION

MATISSE'S FIRST EXPERIENCE OF PAINTING was as a twenty-year-old law clerk in 1890, convalescing from appendicitis at his parents' home in the northern French town of Bohain-en-Vermandois. Painting opened for him, he said, a kind of paradise, set apart from the prosaic world. Within a year or so, he had abandoned law and was in Paris studying painting.

His earliest works were dark still lifes in a manner ultimately derived from Dutch naturalism. At the École des Beaux-Arts in Paris, he made academic studies from plaster casts and from posed models, and he copied pictures at the Louvre. While he rejected the stultifying conservatism of academic training, its emphasis on representation of the human figure and on deep knowledge of the art of the past would assume great importance for him. In the middle and late 1890s, however, it was modern art that slowly began to engage his attention. The forms in his still lifes began to assume a new radiance, even within their darkly tonal settings, as in *Lemons and Bottle of Dutch Gin,* of 1896 (p. 21), and eventually were broken apart by the influences of Impressionism and Post-Impressionism. Matisse's *Still Life* of 1899 (p. 23) is constructed from areas of color whose descriptive function is only summarily indicated. Paintings such as this have been called "proto-Fauve," for they anticipate what will become Matisse's genius as a colorist: his using color not to imitate light, but to create it.

At turn-of-century, Matisse's interests turned increasingly to the work of Paul Cézanne, whom he would call a "god of painting." Until 1904, an architectonic style concerned with expressing volume as color—through juxtaposed patches of different colors, as in *Male Model,* of c. 1900 (p. 25), or through sculptural masses composed of variations of a single color—dominated his production. Paintings in this style, based mainly on the bodily image, are physically more substantial than any he had done earlier: ruggedly and energetically modeled. Not surprisingly, they

led him to study sculpture. *The Serf,* of 1900–04 (p. 27), was the most important result. Less predictable, perhaps, was his working simultaneously in a variety of other styles during this same period. We see this in his figure drawings, which range from the boldly dissonant to the graceful and tranquil (p. 29). But even the most tranquil are clearly abstractions of the bodily form.

Matisse spent the summer of 1905 working alongside André Derain in the small Mediterranean seaport of Collioure. The paintings they made there, and in Paris on their return, caused a sensation at the Salon d'Automne, in October, when they were exhibited along with works by other of Matisse's acquaintances, including Maurice Vlaminck and Henri Manguin. This group of artists became known as *les fauves* ("the wild beasts") for the supposedly violent appearance of their paintings.

Fauvism meant, as Matisse later said, construction by means of color, and was therefore the source of everything that followed in his art. Color, free from tonal modeling, would be used not to imitate external reality, but rather to convey the artist's response to his subject. The immediacy of that response was embodied in the very immediacy of color, revealing the pure chromatic substance of painting in its most fundamental state. In *Landscape at Collioure* (p. 31) and similar works, he drew with color: with curls and strips of intense reds and greens, and similarly contrasting hues, placed separately on the white ground of the canvas to create a dazzling effect of vibrating light. Often, however, he combined drawn strips of color with broad colored areas, as is beginning to happen in *La japonaise: Woman Beside the Water* (p. 33), and increasingly would use many different kinds of painterly marks within one picture, thus orchestrating the surface with complex harmonies and dissonances. Matisse's drawings and woodcuts of 1905–06 (pp. 35, 37) have a similarly excited charge.

Le bonheur de vivre. Paris, Couvent des Oiseaux, autumn-winter 1905–06. Oil on canvas, 68½" × 7' 9¾" (174 × 238.1 cm). The Barnes Foundation, Merion Station, Pennsylvania.

Le bonheur de vivre (The Happiness of Living), painted in the autumn and winter of 1905–06, brought to an abrupt end the period of visually excited Fauve painting; it offered instead an effect of indolent calm, using broad areas of color bounded by arabesque contours that are reminiscent at times of Ingres and at others of Gauguin to picture a primal world, a Golden Age, populated by images of sexuality. Through 1906, and later, Matisse explored fragments of this world in the form of small figural sculptures (p. 39), some of which would be placed in still lifes that, therefore, resembled pastoral landscapes with figures. He also developed in drawing a style of arabesque contours, making the first of the graceful, pure line drawings (p. 41) and prints (p. 37) that would become so associated with him and that would, eventually, contribute enormously to his popular reputation.

In 1907, the year that saw renewed interest in Paris in the work of Cézanne, and when Pablo Picasso painted *Les demoiselles d'Avignon* (The Museum of Modern Art, New York), Matisse moved against the current of contemporary art. He decisively set aside the sculptural implications of Cézanne's paintings, which would attract the Cubists, and ruthlessly expelled signs of overt dissonance, which contribute to the radical nature of Picasso's masterpiece. Increasingly, he would summarize and flatten the painted figure into surface pattern, as in *Music (oil sketch),* of 1907 (p. 43). Fauvism had been a return to the fundamentals of pictorial expression; it came to require the very simplest means. During a trip to Italy in the summer of 1907, Matisse saw the work of Giotto and other early Renaissance painters. This confirmed for him the path he had chosen. The forementioned painting, and others done around the same time, are simpler and more decorative works than any he had done before. And their subjects evoke the allegories of Renaissance art, while remaining mysteriously resistant to any single explanation.

In "Notes of a Painter," written in 1908, Matisse described his aim as an artist: to discover the "essential character" of things beneath their superficial appearances, thus to produce "an art of balance, of purity and serenity," decorative in conception and expressive of his emotional reactions to the subjects he painted. His *Bather,* of 1909 (p. 45), with its vibrant blue surface and highly simplified figure, exemplifies the decorative aspect of his art. Works of this kind move fully beyond the fragmented surfaces of Fauvism to give to color an even greater reality of its own; it floods over the frontal plane of the canvas, submerging details of things. The form of Matisse's representation is determined by the movement of areas of colored paint.

Color being the primary substance of his art, form was "modified according to the interaction of neighboring colors," Matisse said. Thus the color was "proportionate to the form." The *Bather* was conceived in the tradition begun by the fresco paintings of Giotto, but Matisse remade that tradition in so extreme and simplified a way that his paintings looked barbaric to many of his contemporaries. They were antithetical, certainly, to Cubism, which emerged in this same period— not only in their emphasis on color, but also in their preservation of the wholeness of the human figure. For Matisse, the unity and integrity of the work of art were analogous to those of the figure itself. Thus, sculpture continued to fascinate him. But he sculpted in the manner of a painter, he said; that is, he made visual images in this physical medium, such as *La serpentine* (p. 47), which is composed of solids and voids of equal importance. Thus, his work in sculpture clarified for his painting the visual organization of form.

It was in this period, in fact, that Matisse began his two most extended sculptural projects: the series of five Jeannette heads that occupied him from 1910 to 1916 (pp. 51, 53) and the four Back reliefs that he made on separate occasions from 1908–09 to 1931 (pp. 55, 57, 59, 61). In both series, the process of condensation and abstraction that characterized his paintings is made visible in the changes from one state of the work to the next. Both were accompanied by drawings (pp. 49, 56) that further enlarge our understanding of this process; one of the drawings is, additionally, among his masterpieces in its medium.

In 1911, Matisse's art changed, in part due to the influence of Persian miniatures, in part as a result of the steadily increasing simplification of his means over the previous five years. Some paintings of 1911 take on a new freedom and looseness of paint application. *View of Collioure and the Sea* (p. 63) is so warmly atmospheric as to disguise its compositional simplicity. *Still Life with Aubergines* (p. 65) returns to a "Fauvist" spontaneity of brushwork, but in a more delicate coloration and thinner application, to create an aerated effect. In contrast, *The Red Studio* (p. 67), one of the four great "symphonic" interiors Matisse made that year, suspends separated incidents within a field of color flatter than any painted since Giotto, but nevertheless open to the eye, which travels from one part of the picture to the next as if on a journey through time.

The following year, Matisse made two trips to Morocco and found there—in its landscape, as seen in *Periwinkles* (p. 69), and in the brightly colored costumes of its people—what seemed to him a literal equivalent of the decorative harmony he had been pursuing. This allowed him to return to nature, he said. The paintings

Matisse in his studio at Issy-les-Moulineaux, May 1913, at work on The Back (II). *Photograph by Alvin Langdon Coburn.*

that Matisse made in France between these two trips, including *Goldfish and Sculpture* (p. 71), address the contrast of art and nature by juxtaposing floral motifs with representations of his own works of art, which are seen in the room dedicated to study of that contrast, the artist's studio. In Morocco itself, his painting reached the apogee of decorativeness and artificiality; yet it also began to become more searchingly empirical. The intuitively worked, colored surface conveys the vividness of external reality, experienced as a luminous, harmonic field.

The period of Matisse's art from 1913 to 1917—after his second trip to Morocco and before he moved to Nice—is a time of restless experimentation that produced often severe, highly abstracted, and even geometrically constructed paintings lacking the hedonistic exuberance normally associated with his art. The work of these years is said to reflect the influence of Cubism; Matisse was in contact with artists such as Picasso and Juan Gris and did acknowledge that he used "the methods of modern construction" when painting the *Still Life after Jan Davidsz. de Heem's "La desserte"*, in 1915 (p. 83). This period's work is also said to reflect the anxieties of World War I. Both explanations are reasonable. And yet, what Matisse made during these years is not as anomalous as it appears at first sight. He pursues his perennial aim of uncovering the "essential qualities" of things beneath their ephemeral, external appearances. Only now, he radically decomposes the very structure of things in order to uncover their essence, and the symbols that result are more ruthless in their simplification than ever before.

The continuity of Matisse's purpose is also made evident by his return to earlier, unfinished projects. Thus, this period opens in 1913 with the second of the Back sculptures and will close in 1916, after the third Back is made and the Jeannette series of sculptures is finally completed. In these new works Matisse either dissects the figure into separate compositional units or reduces it to an ominously elemental state, a minimal diagram of human presence. A similarly diagrammatic quality, and composition from isolated units, is to be found in paintings of this period, from *The Blue Window*, of 1913 (p. 73), to *Gourds*, of 1915–16 (p. 87).

Given Matisse's preoccupation with the human figure, it is not surprising that some of the most extraordinary works of the period are portraits. These include very untraditional pictures, like *Woman on a High Stool (Germaine Raynal)*, of 1914 (p. 75), which evokes an almost penitential mood that stifles without quite canceling an innate sensuality. Others, however, notably drawings and etchings (p. 79), are carefully observed works of often extreme delicacy.

Occasional paintings of this period are so boldly simplified that their subjects are almost indecipherable, as with *View of Notre-Dame* (p. 77) and *Goldfish and Palette* (p. 81), both made in 1914. But even these clearly derive from external reality. In the latter, Matisse revises and reduces the subject into schematic patterns of analogous forms, while miraculously maintaining

a description of the natural fall of light. As ever, structure is the result of, and recalls, visual experience. Even the highly geometrized *Piano Lesson,* of 1916 (p. 89), is thus a naturalistic picture as well as an abstract one. The same is true of *The Rose Marble Table,* of 1917 (p. 91), as simply silhouetted as one of the paper cutouts Matisse would make much later; yet here the appearance of nature presses more insistently upon our attention. It signals a change.

At the end of 1917, Matisse moved, alone, to Nice. He would live in Nice and its environs for at least part, and usually most, of each year for the remainder of his life. However, it is the span of years through the 1920s that is usually known as his "Nice period." During this time, he painted the harmonious, light-filled, and often profusely decorated interiors, with languorous and seductive models, that sacrificed the interest of the avant-garde, an interest he regained only slowly in later years.

Matisse rejoiced in the light of Nice; color was subordinated to it. Thus, the flat, arbitrary colors of his paintings since 1906 were replaced by a much broader range of soft tonalities that convey how reflected light will suffuse an interior, associating whatever or whoever is within it. Light is almost palpable in paintings like *Interior with a Violin Case,* of 1918–19 (p. 93). Their sensuality and the quality of meditation they afford both depend on the gentle pulsation of light through them. Often, the pulsation of pattern will form an accompaniment. The world of these paintings therefore appears indolent and becalmed. But it also seems extremely artificial; the rooms, their decoration, the costumes of the models are all a form of make-believe. The paradisal world that Matisse previously only imagined is here made real. The naturalism of these paintings is therefore not ironic (as was that of Picasso and others at this time), but sincere and entirely unashamed.

The experience of drawing was particularly crucial to what Matisse was doing. At times, most notably with the famous *Plumed Hat*

Matisse drawing a model at no. 1, place Charles-Félix, Nice, c. 1927–28.

drawings, of 1919 (p. 95), it produces a more detailed counterpoint to the paintings. At others, it explores their tonal underpinnings, as with the extraordinary, vividly illusionistic lithographs of these years (pp. 97, 99, 107). And at yet others, it recovers the pure contours of objects and figures, transforming them into sensual patterns in pen-and-ink drawings and etchings (pp. 103, 105) whose principal subject is the odalisque. In the second half of the decade, though, sculpture came to preoccupy the artist once again, and he produced his largest freestanding work in this medium. *Large Seated Nude*, of 1925–29 (p. 101), is developed from the pose of an odalisque (p. 97), but gains in solidity and bulk, in sharpness of definition, and in the extent of its formalization. By the end of the decade, Matisse would be saying, "I want a certain formal perfection." And naturalism retreated before it.

Matisse stopped making easel paintings in 1929, not fully to begin again until 1934–35. Some of his most original works in this medium were yet to be created, but never again did the very practice of painting have quite the same absolute priority as before. Painting increasingly became a means for releasing the presence of color, conceived as if some pure and independent element, aloof even from the means of its application.

The return to formal simplicity around 1930 returned Matisse to the kind of clarity he had achieved in works made twenty years earlier; but much had changed. The sensuality of his paintings of the 1920s had resided as much in the settings of the figures as in the figures themselves. What attracted Matisse in the 1930s was how he could form clear-cut figures into an expanding surface pattern by giving equal weight to the spaces between them. As usual, a change was accompanied by work in sculpture. Around 1931, Matisse made the last of his Back sculptures (p. 61) and smaller works (p. 109) that condense the figure into simple patterns of analogous forms.

His drawings were critically affected by the new preoccupations. They became clearer

and more condensed than at any earlier time. At the beginning of the decade, the etchings Matisse made to illustrate an edition of Stéphane Mallarmé's poems (p. 111) had an almost neoclassical quality to their elegant, filament-like lines—a quality fully appropriate to the mythological themes from antiquity that they introduced into Matisse's art of this period. It became his practice to rehearse such simplified line drawings by making works in charcoal. These show us the very process of condensation, as a figure is reduced to its essential structure (p. 113). Matisse continued to make both simplified line drawings and exploratory charcoal drawings in the 1940s (pp. 115, 119). And his interest in book illustration developed in concert. (In 1941, illness and then surgery made painting difficult for him.) The linoleum-cut plates for *Pasiphaé*, of 1944 (p. 117), take another mythological subject into the realm of patterned abstraction.

Matisse spoke of "the eternal conflict of drawing and color." The different periods of his long career show differing forms of reciprocation between these two basic pictorial elements. The paper cutout maquettes he made in the early 1940s for his illustrated book *Jazz* (pp. 121–123) revealed to him a novel way of actually conflating these elements. "Instead of drawing an outline and filling in the color . . . I am drawing directly in color," he said. Drawing with scissors—cutting shapes from paper that was prepainted—meant that the contour of a shape and its internal area were formed simultaneously. The large ink drawings of the 1940s and early 1950s, done with a broad brush (pp. 125, 127), afforded precisely the same symbiosis of contour and internal area in each stroke. Matisse thought of them as a new kind of monochrome painting. They were accompanied by aquatints of a comparable boldness (p. 129).

Eventually, brush drawings and cutouts formed virtually his only means of expression. The walls of his studios began to fill with sheets of boldly simplified drawings and loosely pinned-up

Matisse's bedroom at the Hôtel Régina, Nice-Cimiez, c. 1952, with paper cutout maquettes for the Vence chapel chasubles on the wall. On the mantel, at center, is Picasso's Winter Landscape, *of 1950, on loan to Matisse. Above the door at the left is* Woman in a Blue Gandoura Robe, *of 1951, and on the floor to the right of the mantel is* Katia, *of 1951. These are Matisse's last two paintings.*

shapes of colored paper resembling leaves, algae, coral, and the like, a sort of imaginary garden to be harvested for making a new kind of work of art. In 1946, Matisse had made his first large-scale cutouts. Toward the end of the decade, cutouts were used to design windows for the Chapel of the Rosary of the Dominican Nuns, at Vence, and, in 1950–52, for the priests' chasubles (p. 133), while his complementary medium, brush drawing, was used to design ceramic-tile murals for the chapel. Matisse made other cutouts as maquettes for decorative projects, ranging from new stained-glass window designs (p. 143) to book covers (p. 131). But he also made them as independent works. The largest and most ambitious of these was the environmental *Swimming Pool* (pp. 140–141), which originally occupied the walls of his dining room. It conflates a sense of color carved into substantial shape with an effect of soaring movement that escapes the limitations of the physical, even the limitations of the pictorial frame. His last style,

like the last styles of other great artists, amounts to a coincidence of opposites. The hypnotic integrity of the interior space and the energy that is released into our space are inseparable and interfused.

Matisse had been born on 31 December 1869, at Le Cateau-Cambrésis in the north of France, and, as we learned at the beginning of this introduction, made his first paintings in 1890. He died on 3 November 1954, in Nice, and was working up to the time of his death, at age eighty-four. His artistic career thus spanned some six-and-a-half decades. The foregoing account of it is aimed at providing a broad context for appreciation of works in the collection of The Museum of Modern Art, and for the discussions of these works in the pages that follow. No short introduction, of course, can possibly provide more than an outline of the richness and plenitude of the work of this most extraordinary of modern artists.

TITLES OF WORKS. Wherever possible, the titles given here are the earliest published titles on record, unless superseded by others that became established within Matisse's lifetime. A diagonal slash (/) is used to divide two alternative titles when both became established in Matisse's lifetime and remain in common use. Parentheses enclosing numerals indicate that these numerals were not part of the original title. Titles placed in square brackets are the earliest published titles on record.

PLACES AND DATES OF EXECUTION. Places of execution are given by city and, when known, by the name of Matisse's residence or studio. Dates of execution are given by year, preceded by season, where known, except for works that are dated more precisely by their inscriptions.

Any part of either the place or date of execution enclosed in square brackets indicates that no firm documentation (such as references in contemporaneous letters or accounts, or inscriptions on the work itself) exists for this information, and that it represents, rather, what our research indicates to be probable. Where there is less certainty as to the date of a work, the designation "c." for *circa* is also used; where we have proposed or adopted a particularly speculative date, a question mark is used.

Dates for sculpture refer to the date of execution of the original clay or plaster model.

MEDIUMS AND DIMENSIONS. Drawings and prints are on white or near-white paper. The description "gouache on paper, cut and pasted" is used for Matisse's cutouts to indicate that the paper in these works was pre-painted by the artist or his assistants. Dimensions are given in inches and (in parentheses) in centimeters; height precedes width, followed, in the case of sculpture, by depth. Unless otherwise specified, drawings and cutouts are works on paper, for which sheet sizes are given. For prints, plate or composition sizes also appear.

INSCRIPTIONS. Inscriptions are shown in the precise form in which they appear on the works, and their locations are indicated. In the case of sculpture, in order to avoid detailed descriptions of the location, only the inscription itself is generally listed. Where a founder is known, that information follows the inscription.

COLLECTIONS. All works in this book are in the collection of The Museum of Modern Art. We have indicated former collections when the objects in question previously belonged to major early collectors of Matisse's work or were in private collections for which important published catalogues exist. This information, however, is necessarily highly selective.

HENRI MATISSE: Masterworks from The Museum of Modern Art

Lemons and Bottle of Dutch Gin

Les citrons et la bouteille de Schiedam

Paris, [early] 1896
Oil on canvas, 12¼ × 11½" (31.2 × 29.3 cm)
Signed and dated lower left: "H. Matisse.96"
The Museum of Modern Art, New York.
Gift of Mr. and Mrs. Warren Brandt

The first original paintings that Matisse made were still lifes, created in 1890. It was as a still-life painter that Matisse first began to make a reputation, in 1896, the date of this painting. And it was as such a painter that he first began to assimilate modernism, and to provoke hostile criticism, in the following year.

Still life is necessarily an evocative form that gains meaning from the artist's choice of objects to represent. In Matisse's early paintings, this choice often evokes domesticity and the closed, secure world of the bourgeois family. He would later talk of wanting to "animate with [his] own feelings" whatever he painted; the inherent passivity of still life was, therefore, a constant attraction, and eventually provided him with the means of presenting in condensed form often highly complex iconographic schemes. It would be wrong, however, to see much more in the lemons and the glass of transparent liquid of this painting than an early use of objects that continued to fascinate him.

Although the confrontation of Dutch realist setting and the already quite radiant fruit and glass may be viewed in retrospect as a source for what these objects would later often evoke—a feeling of sensual release from immediate reality to something more basic and eternal even than domesticity—they still belong, at this moment, to the bourgeois world. If these objects relate at all to another world, it is through the light that enters the interior to heighten their color and luster (more than their volume), thus drawing them apart from the surrounding gloom. Even in Matisse's earliest work, it is light that transforms and idealizes material things.

Still Life
Nature morte

Paris, [early 1899]
Oil on canvas, 18⅛ × 15" (46 × 38.1 cm)
Signed lower left: "Henri Matisse"
The Museum of Modern Art, New York.
Gift of A. Conger Goodyear

In 1898–99, during a lengthy trip to Ajaccio, in Corsica, and then to the region around Toulouse, Matisse's paintings, especially the still lifes, became increasingly bold in their use of vivid, arbitrary colors; these works were thus subsequently considered "proto-Fauve." This painting, probably made in Paris upon his return, is continuous with those "breakthrough" canvases. Like them, it shows his liberation from the constraints of naturalism to achieve a spontaneous, indeed at times reckless, interpretation of Impressionist idioms.

The pictorial pretext is naturalistic: Matisse concerns himself with rendering the light falling on objects. But he transposes this into two-dimensional and coloristic terms. His colleague Jean Puy recalled that Matisse chose to use bold colors and to emphasize the materiality of his painting "in order to produce the maximum resonance on the eye." This "resonance," which becomes characteristic of Matisse's paintings, is of course anti-naturalistic. As he would say later, the issue was not of representing the objects set up as a still life. "This spectacle creates a shock in my mind. That is what I have to represent."

When Matisse started to teach, he distinguished between the Impressionist method of "considering color as warm and cool" and a different method, "seeking light through the opposition of colors." By the date of this painting, he had already learned that the light produced by contrasts seemed more exact to inner experience, and more lasting, than that which represented the flux of the world. He knew then, he said, that he had discovered his "true path."

Male Model
L'homme nu

Paris, [c. 1900]
Oil on canvas, 39⅛ × 28⅝" (99.3 × 72.7 cm)
Not signed, not dated
The Museum of Modern Art, New York.
Kay Sage Tanguy and Abby Aldrich Rockefeller Funds

Matisse made very few figure studies before 1900. Once established, however, this subject matter became his major preoccupation. "What interests me most is neither still life nor landscape, but the human figure," he would write in his famous "Notes of a Painter" of 1908. "It is that which best permits me to express my so-to-speak religious attitude toward life." Making reference to works such as this, which show an Italian model named Bevilacqua, he continued: "I do not insist upon all the details of the face, on setting them down one by one with anatomical exactitude. . . . A work of art must carry within itself its complete significance and impose that upon the beholder even before he recognizes the subject." Hence, while the linked succession of planes on the torso describes the muscularity of the figure, it also possesses an intrinsic interest at least equivalent to that of the subject itself.

The blue tonality of the *Male Model* may well owe something to the Bather compositions of Paul Cézanne, one of which Matisse purchased in 1899. Yet he was less interested in the specific color choices of Cézanne than in the architectonic structure that Cézanne created from color. The weight and gravity of this figure, its sober, impassive expression, and its immobile pose all closely relate it to Cézanne's studies of the nude, as well as illustrating Matisse's conviction (as given in "Notes of a Painter") that "expression . . . does not reside in passions flaring up in a human face or manifested by violent movement. The entire arrangement of my picture is expressive."

The Serf
Le serf

Paris, [1900–04]
Bronze, 37⅜ × 13⅜ × 13" (92.3 × 34.5 × 33 cm)
Inscribed: "Henri Matisse" and "Le Serf"
Founder, A. Bingen-Costenoble
The Museum of Modern Art, New York.
Mr. and Mrs. Sam Salz Fund

Matisse himself was explicit about the role of sculpture in his art as a whole: "I took up sculpture," he said, "because what interested me in painting was a clarification of my ideas. I changed my method and worked in clay in order to have a rest from painting, where I had done all I could for the time being. That is to say it was done for the purposes of organization, to put order into my feelings, and find a style to suit me. When I found it in sculpture, it helped me in my painting. It was always in view of a complete possession of my mind, a sort of hierarchy of my sensations, that I kept on working in the hope of finding an ultimate solution."

The Serf was Matisse's first important sculpture. Begun in the same year as the *Male Model* (p. 25), it shows the model, Bevilacqua, in the same pose as in that painting. Bevilacqua had been one of Auguste Rodin's models, and *The Serf* is Matisse's most Rodinesque sculpture—but only superficially so, for it revises Rodin's heroic monumentality to create something far more aesthetically contained. Matisse had recognized that his work discipline was already the reverse of Rodin's. Unlike Rodin, Matisse did not model clay as an analogy of flesh; he avoided both a mimetic surface and the depiction of the effect of internal anatomy upon the surface. He explained: "Already I could only envisage the general architecture of a work of mine, replacing explanatory details by a living and suggestive synthesis." Still, the fact that this sculpture took several *hundred* sessions to make suggests that it was only with difficulty that Matisse achieved such a synthesis.

Study for "Madeleine (I)"
Étude pour "Madeleine (I)"

Paris, [c. 1901]
Pencil on paper, 11¾ × 9¼" (29.6 × 23.4 cm)
Estate stamp lower right: "H. Matisse"
The Museum of Modern Art, New York.
Gift of Mr. and Mrs. Pierre Matisse in honor and memory of Victor Leventritt

Study of a Standing Nude, Her Arm Covering Her Face
Étude de femme nue debout, bras cachant le visage

Paris, [c. 1901–03]
Brush and pen and ink on paper, 10⅜ × 8" (26.4 × 20.3 cm)
Signed lower right: "Henri-Matisse"
The Museum of Modern Art, New York.
Gift of Edward Steichen

Of these two drawings, that in pencil is a study for Matisse's 1901 sculpture *Madeleine (I)*. Although the sculpture shows a figure that has been thinned since the drawing, and formed into an almost Art Nouveau arabesque, the drawing rehearses its classical pose of equilibrium, with the weight resting on one leg and the other leg bent as if to move. Matisse clearly understood how the contrast produced by this pose between the long, undulating, relaxed side of the body and the arched swing of the hip on the opposite side, the *déhanchement*, had always been a potent symbol of desire. Yet the figure seems self-protective in its posture; less open to desire than resisting it.

The same may be said, even more, of the roughly contemporaneous ink drawing, whose subject shields her face against the beholder. If the former work is still tender in its draftsmanship, and therefore evocative of sensual attention, this is an aggressively dissonant work in which the abrasive marks of a reed pen cut out the image from the ground under the pretense of depicting shadow. The figure thus reads as almost an absence in the sheet, as unavailable to us as her pose signals that she is. Volume as such is indicated by areas of blank, white paper; concavities and spaces by strokes of the pen. This led Matisse's fellow students—with whom he was sharing his models—to remark that he was making a "negative" (in the photographic sense) of what he saw. The model, shielding her face, makes herself invisible to positive attention, and hence unobtainable.

Landscape at Collioure
Paysage à Collioure

Collioure, [summer 1905]
Oil on canvas, 15⅜ × 18¼" (39 × 46.2 cm)
Signed lower left: "Henri Matisse"
The Museum of Modern Art, New York.
Gift of Mrs. Bertram Smith

The paintings that Matisse made in the summer of 1905 in the small Mediterranean port of Collioure, not far from the Spanish border, were among those that gave his circle the name *les fauves*, "the wild beasts," when his and his colleagues' works were exhibited in Paris, in the Salon d'Automne of that year.

Matisse's paintings of that summer were wilder, more reckless than any he subsequently produced in his career. He responded impetuously to the intense light of the south, threw off the constraints of drawing, and pursued color for its own sake. Color without drawing meant landscape. It was therefore in landscape painting that Matisse's crucial breakthroughs in the use of color occurred. The result, though, was an unexpected one. Color without drawing led to drawing with color, the structural basis of the present painting.

It is a veritable flurry of brushstrokes whose varying directions are all that tell us we are seeing a path through trees with a hill in the far distance. There is possibly a strip of blue water beyond the end of the path as it disappears over the brow of the hill, but color is no guarantee of identity here, for the trees, too, are liberally dosed with multiple colors. Only the direction of the colored marks conveys a description. Thus, paint is drawn in the painting. Color does not describe. But it creates light—of the most vibrant, dazzling kind—from contrasts of primaries that reach across their separation by the beige-white of the canvas. Seeking light through the opposition of colors, and drawing in color to shape it, would become Matisse's persistent aim.

La japonaise: Woman Beside the Water
La japonaise au bord de l'eau

Collioure, summer 1905
Oil and pencil on canvas, 13⅞ × 11⅛" (35.2 × 28.2 cm)
Signed lower left: "Henri-Matisse"
The Museum of Modern Art, New York.
Purchase and partial anonymous gift
Formerly collection Michael and Sarah Stein

This painting shows Matisse's wife wearing a Japanese costume, seated beside the ocean at Collioure. At least, that is the nominal subject. The figure is decomposed in its painting and merges with the landscape around it.

Color, being released from representation of the substance of things, is also released from the obligation to render tonal distinctions. In the absence of tonal tissue, Matisse gives us the colored skeleton of a subject, and a loosely articulated one at that. He refuses to exactly define the spaces between the parts of the subject. Leaving the links open was to charge the fixed image with a feeling of potential movement, and to thereby free it from the temporal moment from which it derived. Fauvism, Matisse insisted, was more than merely bright color. "That is only the surface; what characterized Fauvism was that we rejected imitative colors, and that with pure colors we obtained stronger reactions—more striking simultaneous reactions." The simultaneous retinal reactions of multiple, juxtaposed colors, vibrating against the white ground, is what blurs the figural image so that it seems to fuse into the landscape. The substance of the figure is corroded in the visual flux.

And yet, the visual flux harks back to the figure it is corroding. Madame Matisse sits there, or floats, rather, her gown even more aquatic in its pattern than the ocean behind her. We know that her husband admired Japanese prints. His wife, as pictured here, recalls a famous seventeenth-century commentator on such prints, who spoke of "a gourd floating along with the river current: this is what we call the *floating world.*"

Jeanne Manguin

Paris, [autumn 1905–spring 1906]

Brush and reed pen and ink on paper,
24½ × 18½" (62.2 × 46.9 cm)
Signed lower right: "Henri-Matisse"
The Museum of Modern Art, New York.
Given anonymously

This magnificent portrait of Jeanne Manguin, the wife of one of Matisse's fellow Fauve artists, is tangibly present to us: close and vividly real. It is indeed a portrait, not simply a drawing of a model. The character of the figuration solidly engages an intimate, unidealized, and manifestly human presence. We are utterly convinced that Matisse knew this young woman; that she sat, just there, opposite him, carefully overdressed for the occasion. And whether the wry irony subverting the modishness of the pose was in the dressing as well as the drawing (we suspect it was), we do enjoy it in the drawing, for the sense of collusive intimacy that it provides brings us even closer to this highly sympathetic portrayal.

What comes almost instantaneously upon our engagement with this figure, however, is the curiously illusive nature of her physical presence. She is indeed tangibly real to us, but the drawing is strangely devoid of a whole range of tactile connotations. Its facture is remarkable. Although partly indebted to Vincent van Gogh, the sheer variety of marks, lines, spots, scribbles, and summary shading produced by the brush and the reed pen makes a virtue of its inconsistency in a truly radical way. Matisse exaggerates discordant facture as never quite before, seeking to rebuild the represented subject from the chaos of sensations, and in that rebuilding to discover its emotional content. But far from varying his handling to focus attention on psychologically expressive features like face or hands, he deflects it from them to spread "expression" through every part of the figure, and of the work.

Large Nude
Le grand nu

[Paris, early 1906 or early 1907?]
Lithograph, printed in black: composition 11³⁄₁₆ ×
9¹⁵⁄₁₆" (28.5 × 25.3 cm); sheet 17¹¹⁄₁₆ × 13⅞" (45 × 35.3 cm)
Signed lower right in pencil: "37/50/Henri-Matisse"
The Museum of Modern Art, New York.
Gift of Abby Aldrich Rockefeller (by exchange)

Seated Nude
Nu assis/Petit bois clair

Paris, [early 1906]
Woodcut, printed in black: composition 13⁷⁄₁₆ ×
10⁷⁄₁₆" (34.2 × 26.6 cm); sheet 18¹⁄₁₆ × 11¼"
(46 × 28.4 cm)
Signed lower left on the block: "HM" and lower
right in pencil: "Henri-Matisse"
The Museum of Modern Art, New York.
Abby Aldrich Rockefeller Fund

Pensive Nude in Folding Chair
Figure pensive au fauteuil pliant

Paris, [early 1906]
Lithograph, printed in black: composition 14¾ ×
10⁹⁄₁₆" (37.4 × 26.9 cm); sheet: 17¹¹⁄₁₆ × 11" (45 × 28 cm)
Signed lower right on the stone: "HM-" and lower
right in ink: "21/25"
The Museum of Modern Art, New York.
Given anonymously, in memory of Leo and Nina
Stein

Seated Nude
Nu assis/Le grand bois

Paris, [early 1906]
Woodcut, printed in black: composition 18¹¹⁄₁₆ ×
14¹⁵⁄₁₆" (47.5 × 38 cm); sheet 22⅝ × 18¹⁄₁₆" (57.5 × 46 cm)
Signed lower left on the block: "hm" and lower
right in ink: "Henri-Matisse 33/50"
The Museum of Modern Art, New York.
Gift of Mr. and Mrs. R. Kirk Askew, Jr.

Matisse's first woodcuts and lithographs were made in the same months that he worked on his large arcadian composition *Le bonheur de vivre* and were exhibited in his second one-man exhibition, in March 1906. They show that he was using the condensed, synthetic form of linear composition of *Le bonheur de vivre*, only applying it to the test of recording the observed, not the invented, world.

The boldness and refinement displayed in these works, four of which are shown here, go far beyond what Matisse had so far attempted in printmaking. In the case of most of the lithographs he begins to incorporate the flowing, uninterrupted line that characterizes much of his subsequent drawing. (In fact, the purely linear lithographs, which show the same model, derive from drawings on transfer paper.) With the woodcuts, which also show this model, he begins to articulate space as an accumulation of patterned areas that lock together to form a decoration. (These woodcuts were cut by Madame Matisse following her husband's brush-and-ink drawings.)

The more densely worked lithograph *Large Nude*, Matisse's first attempt at working directly upon the lithographic stone, is an anomaly in this group. It was certainly done on a separate occasion from that of the other lithographs. Some have even suggested that it belongs with Matisse's Cubist-influenced work of the teens. Yet it is a generalized version of the pose seen in the woodcut *Seated Nude*, known as *Le grand bois*, a transformation of that sleeping figure into an image of utter unconsciousness.

Standing Nude, Arms on Head
Nu debout, bras sur la tête

Paris or Collioure, [1906]
Bronze, 10⅜ × 4⅛ × 4⅞" (26.2 × 10.2 × 12.3 cm)
Inscribed: "Henri Matisse/10"
Founder, C. Valsuani
The Museum of Modern Art, New York.
Gift of Mrs. Bertram Smith

Seated Figure, Right Hand on Ground
Nu assis, main droite à terre

[Paris, 1908]
Bronze, 7½ × 5⅜ × 4⅜" (19 × 13.7 × 11.2 cm)
Inscribed: "7/10 HM"
Founder, C. Valsuani
The Museum of Modern Art, New York.
Abby Aldrich Rockefeller Fund

Standing Nude, Arms on Head and *Seated Figure, Right Hand on Ground* belong to a sequence of miniature sculptures that Matisse made in the period 1900–08. All of Matisse's sculptures, with the exception of the Back sculptures (pp. 55, 57, 59, 61) and *Large Seated Nude* (p. 101), are of modest dimensions, for he demanded an intimate and nonrhetorical scale, as well as feeling, for his work in this medium. The reason for this was not only that the sculptures were made as private objects, for clarifying ideas, rather than as public manifestos, nor only that they were conceived for domestic or studio settings. Smallness of scale also allowed Matisse the very direct engagement that he needed with the sculptural medium in order to realize the essential rhythms observed in the model in the most immediate, forthright, and specific way; and the sensation of volume could most intensely be expressed in works of graspable proportions, works that could be enclosed within the hand.

"A sculpture must invite us to handle it as an object," Matisse told his students, "just as the sculptor must feel, in making it, the particular demands for volume and mass. The smaller the piece of sculpture, the more the essentials of form must exist." With these two small sculptures, not only the surface of the works but their very forms seem to have been shaped by the pressure of the artist's hand. The original clay was rolled and bent, pushed and prodded, and maintained its materiality as Matisse took it just barely to the point of figural representation.

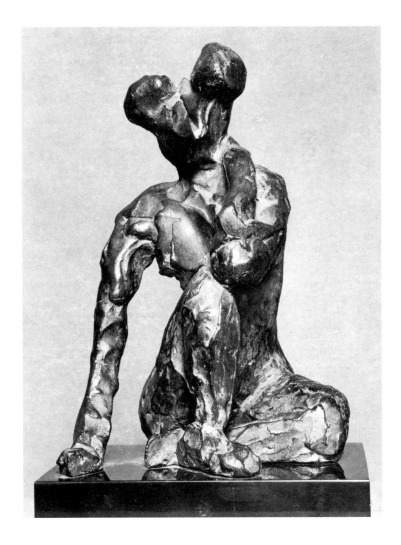

Marguerite Reading
Marguerite lisant

[Collioure, 1906]
Pen and ink on paper, 15⅝ × 20½" (39.6 × 52.1 cm)
Signed lower right: "Henri-Matisse"
The Museum of Modern Art, New York.
Acquired through the Lillie P. Bliss Bequest

Marguerite Reading, a portrait of Matisse's daughter made in the summer of 1906, during his second visit to Collioure, exemplifies his justly celebrated, highly economical style of pen-and-ink drawing, which emerged in his art that year. He had made spare line drawings before this date, but only in 1906 do they achieve the level of refinement and condensation that we find here.

As with the contemporaneous prints (p. 37), this drawing reveals the impact of the linear style of *Le bonheur de vivre*. And, like those prints, it shows a figure that is self-absorbed. *Le bonheur de vivre* had pictured an idealized world set apart from ordinary reality. One of the subsequent tasks that Matisse set himself was to evoke such a feeling of self-enclosure in subjects observed in the real world. Here, his daughter seems distanced in the realm of her own thoughts and feelings, which contributes to the tender vulnerability of this beautiful drawing.

It is at once a whole image and an accumulation of parts suspended from the top of the sheet. Reading the whole image requires reassembling the parts: the ribbon that floats in the hair, the hair falling on the forehead, the curls of hair on the shoulders, the parallel lines marking the neckline of the dress, and the cluster of heavier lines that shows the profile within the three-quarter view. Putting the image together, we see that it forms a sequence of spatial compartments that design the shape of the paper, and that its abstractness is of a kind that admits even the most delicate of details, like the tiny strokes of the pen that mark the eyelashes on the closed lids of the eyes.

Music (oil sketch)
La musique (esquisse)

Collioure, spring–summer 1907
Oil on canvas, 29 × 24" (73.4 × 60.8 cm)
Signed lower left: "Henri Matisse"
The Museum of Modern Art, New York.
Gift of A. Conger Goodyear in honor of Alfred H. Barr, Jr.
Formerly collections Leo and Gertrude Stein; John Quinn

Matisse played the violin, and the standing violinist to the left of this painting is commonly understood to be a surrogate self-portrait. The androgyny of this figure is not unusual among Matisse's decorative, arcadian compositions; the gender of his 1909 *Bather* (p. 45) is almost as indefinite. The artist appeared to have welcomed the ambiguity. Besides, no other figure in the painting appears to notice it, for they seem utterly absorbed in the music, either quietly listening or dancing in passionate embrace. To interpret the violinist as the artist estranged from both the calming and the enlivening results of his art would cast an anxious mood on the painting that is belied by its fresh and candid charm. Yet themes of frustration and alienation are inherent to the subject of arcadia, if only because such a carefree world no longer exists. Such themes, expressed in the compositional isolation of figures, manifest themselves in subsequent paintings by Matisse, including *Music* of 1910 (State Hermitage Museum, St. Petersburg), in which the figure of the standing violinist is repeated.

Insofar as Matisse entitled the present painting *Music (oil sketch)*, it would seem to be a study for the 1910 composition. Yet when this "sketch" was made, he had not yet received the commission, from Russian merchant Sergei Shchukin, that produced *Music* and its companion painting, *Dance* (also in St. Petersburg). This suggests that well before that commission came, Matisse was already hoping to make a subsequent, more fully developed painting on a musical theme.

Bather

Baigneuse

[Cavalière, summer 1909]
Oil on canvas, 36½ × 29⅛" (92.7 × 74 cm)
Signed lower right: "Henri-Matisse"
The Museum of Modern Art, New York.
Gift of Abby Aldrich Rockefeller

We know that Matisse worked from a female model in the summer during which this *Bather* was painted. But it is uncertain whether this painting was done from a model and whether its subject is a female. The pose derives from a composition of female bathers by Cézanne that Matisse owned, suggesting that his own painting is a synthesis of observed and remembered forms from art and nature.

It also relates to the first of his Back reliefs (p. 55), completed the same year, which similarly examines how a figure may be joined to a vertical plane. In the painting, by identifying the vivid blue ground with the water through which the bather wades, Matisse asks us to imagine it wading through the plane of the picture, too. In seeking to accommodate so weighty, three-dimensional a form to the flattened surface, Matisse reprises a theme previously explored in works like the *Male Model* (p. 25). Once again, he has confronted the basic pictorial problem with which Cézanne also continually struggled. Comparison of the two paintings shows how economically Matisse is now able to express volume—with thick emphatic outlines, summary shading, and bold anatomical simplifications—and how the illusion of volume now seems so embedded in the surface of the work that it cannot be imagined apart from it. Though silhouetted against the blue ground, the figure cannot conceivably be pried away from it; though unmistakably sculptural in connotation, it eludes our sense of grasp.

La serpentine

Issy-les-Moulineaux, autumn 1909
Bronze, 22¼ × 11 × 7½" (56.5 × 28 × 19 cm)
Inscribed: "Henri Matisse 1/10"
The Museum of Modern Art, New York.
Gift of Abby Aldrich Rockefeller

This sculpture was made when Matisse was also working on *Dance*, his large composition for Shchukin. It, too, is an exploration of the figure as arabesque.

La serpentine, however, is in repose, while the figures in *Dance* are in energetic movement. Whereas the figures in a painting could pass their movement on from one to the next, and contain the movement within the prescribed limits of the frame, a sculpture's self-containment had to be built into its very forms. "No lines can go wild," Matisse insisted. "All the lines must close around a center; otherwise your drawing cannot exist as a unit, for these fleeting lines carry the attention away—they do not arrest it." Here, Matisse contains the arabesque by using the base of the sculpture and the post on which the figure leans to "frame" the serpentine image. This effect offsets the manual, graspable character of the figural volumes, lightens them visually to become aesthetic variables of the enclosed space that they articulate.

Volume becomes line, yet it continues to invite touch, and with that invitation comes a sensual appeal. Only, sensuality is here compressed into the charged coils of the sinuous pose, whose energy is never released, but is contained, coiling around the sculpture on all sides. *La serpentine* was based on a photograph of a model "a little fat but very harmonious in form and movement," Matisse said. "I thinned and composed the forms so that the movement would be completely comprehensible from all points of view."

Girl with Tulips (Jeanne Vaderin)
Jeune fille aux tulipes (Jeanne Vaderin)

Issy-les-Moulineaux, [early 1910]
Charcoal on paper, 28¼ × 23" (73 × 58.4 cm)
Estate stamp lower right: "H. Matisse"
The Museum of Modern Art, New York.
Acquired through the Lillie P. Bliss Bequest

Jeanne Vaderin, the subject of this drawing, was also the subject of Matisse's series of five Jeannette sculptures of 1910–16 (pp. 51, 53) and of the 1910 painting *Girl with Tulips*, now in the Hermitage Museum. The simplified, asymmetrical treatment of the head in the drawing relates it to the first two sculptures (1910), and its subject to the contemporaneous painting. But there its affinities end, for it represents a unique conception of this particular motif: the discovery of pictorial analogies between woman and plant, and fusion of the two into a single image.

The lightly drawn, shieldlike form in the top left corner is a clue to the kind of image that Matisse was seeking. It summarizes the shape of the tulip leaves, is repeated in the drawing of the girl's collar, and is also the whole shape of her head. These analogous forms constitute a growing vertical axis that rises to the facing but profile eye, and from this axis bloom the swerving lines that bend from the shoulders and serpentine down to the tulip-shaped hands. The tapered form of the torso is itself a version of the same module as well as an amplification of the pot from which the plant grows. Figure and plant grow together as one organism to that magnificently impassive head, which culminates what must be one of Matisse's, and this century's, greatest drawings. We see how he worried the features of the face until he established the conflation of profile and three-quarter views (as daring as anything in Cubism, and far more understated), and how concerned he was to return from the head the movement that rises there. Hence, those external guide lines that drop to the shoulders and draw in the whole figure, within a now-inverted form of the basic module, to produce a single, dense image of continuous as well as continual growth.

Jeannette (I)

Issy-les-Moulineaux, [early 1910]
Bronze, 13 × 9 × 10" (33 × 22.8 × 25.5 cm)
Inscribed: "0/10 HM"
The Museum of Modern Art, New York.
Acquired through the Lillie P. Bliss Bequest

Jeannette (III)

Issy-les-Moulineaux, [spring 1910–autumn 1911]
Bronze, 23¾ × 10¼ × 11" (60.3 × 26 × 28 cm)
Inscribed: "5/10 HM"
The Museum of Modern Art, New York.
Acquired through the Lillie P. Bliss Bequest

Jeannette (II)

Issy-les-Moulineaux, [early 1910]
Bronze, 10⅜ × 8¼ × 9⅝" (26.2 × 21 × 24.5 cm)
Inscribed: "2/10 HM"
The Museum of Modern Art, New York.
Gift of Sidney Janis

The first two sculptures in this series of five were made in 1910. *Jeannette I*, made from life, shows the model, Jeanne Vaderin, with a full oval face, prominent nose, and sharply defined eyes with heavy eyebrows, much as she appears in the contemporaneous drawing *Girl with Tulips* (p. 49). Matisse also repeated from the drawing the curious asymmetry of the eyes, but he enlarged the eyes themselves and exaggerated the bones of the cheeks to form large oval accents at each side of the nose. This section of the face would continue to engage Matisse's particular attention throughout the series.

Jeannette II, built on a plaster cast of the preceding sculpture, shows the hair more broadly articulated, the eyes more concentrated, and the distracting separate lines of the eyebrows removed, with nose and brow joined into a single dipping profile line. Since we have no reason to believe that in 1910 Matisse had planned the three later sculptures in the series, it seems fair to think of *Jeannette I* and *Jeannette II* as two renderings of the same subject in alternate modes: the first, cool, calm, and more naturalistic; the second, more animated, rougher, and relatively more abstract. To recognize that they thus form a pair leads to the further recognition that the third and the fourth sculptures in the series do so as well. This second pair, moreover, shows the same development from a calmer conception to a more animated one. Thus, the order of the whole series is not only that of its numerical sequence, but is also a dialectical one. The expressiveness of the second sculpture leads to the almost expressionistic fourth sculpture (and not to the more architectonic third). The fifth and final sculpture in the series will develop not from the fourth but from the third, being built on a cast of that third sculpture.

Jeannette (IV)

Issy-les-Moulineaux, [spring 1910–autumn 1911]
Bronze, 24⅛ × 10¾ × 11¼" (61.3 × 27.4 × 28.7 cm)
Inscribed: "5/10 HM"
The Museum of Modern Art, New York.
Acquired through the Lillie P. Bliss Bequest

Jeannette (V)

Issy-les-Moulineaux, [1916]
Bronze, 22⅞ × 8⅜ × 10⅝" (58.1 × 21.3 × 27.1 cm)
Inscribed: "5/10 HM"
The Museum of Modern Art, New York.
Acquired through the Lillie P. Bliss Bequest

With *Jeannette III* and *Jeannette IV*, made in 1910–11, the entire conception of the motif is radically altered. The portrait head is replaced by a three-part structure of head, bust, and sculptural base, reinforced by the rearrangement of the hair into three prominent volumes and by the emphasis given to the triad of eyes and nose. Seen from the front, both sculptures are like stubby columns, or like plants that alternately swell and contract as they grow to the petaled head. In the third sculpture, Matisse begins to create volumes on the basis of what previously read as tonal shifts across the face. Perceived tonality is made sculptural not by effacing it, not by seeking the monolith behind the tonally broken surface, but by exaggerating it, making the perceived breaks in the surface the divisions between separately defined forms. In the more animated fourth sculpture, this is carried to such an extent as to produce the effect of a constructed as well as a modeled composition.

Jeannette V, made in 1916, reasserts the wholeness of the head. It does so, however, by means of the most radical surgery, a kind of surgery that first cuts away the hair and then penetrates into the very core of the head to expose the volumes that compose it. The form of the head is opened into a sequence of broad, knifecut blocks and planes responsive partly to the inherent structure of the face, partly to the effect of illumination upon it, and partly to the autonomous relationship between the blocks and planes themselves. This sculpture is contemporaneous with Matisse's Cubist-affected paintings, including *Piano Lesson* (p. 89), and may usefully be compared to the head of the boy in that painting, which is also penetrated by the ambient space. However, *Jeannette V* is far more ruthless in what it does to the representation and far more concerned with the solidity of the representation, which it clings to even as it threatens to disperse it. Matisse does not simplify and abstract to escape but rather to preserve and intensify what attracted him to the subject in the first place. *Jeannette V* is psychologically as well as sculpturally the strongest and most forceful of the series.

The Back (I)
Nu de dos (I)

Paris, Hôtel Biron, and Issy-les-Moulineaux, spring 1908–late 1909
Bronze, 6' 2⅜" × 44½" × 6½" (188.9 × 113 × 16.5 cm)
Inscribed lower left: "Henri Matisse." Lower right: "H.M./2/10/ 1909"
Founder, C. Valsuani
The Museum of Modern Art, New York.
Mrs. Simon Guggenheim Fund

Matisse's four imposing life-size reliefs, the Back sculptures, were made at widely spaced intervals over a period of more than twenty years, from 1908–09 to c. 1931. They are by far his largest sculptures and, being reliefs, are closer to Matisse's paintings than his fully three-dimensional sculptures. Thus they alone in his sculptural *oeuvre* share with his many grand paintings the look of ambitious, monumental, and public art.

Although they are usually now presented together as a series, where we can judge the remarkable transformation the image undergoes, they were never visible as such in the artist's lifetime. Although they do give the appearance of being conscious public masterpieces, only *Back I* was regularly exhibited by the artist, who late in life did not even remember how many reliefs he had made, and had apparently forgotten entirely about *Back II*, which was only discovered after his death.

The four reliefs were conceived, in fact, in the context of major painting projects, which defined the usefulness of the sculptures to the artist. *Back I* was made in 1908–09, when Matisse was producing such ambitious figure compositions as *Bathers with a Turtle* (The St. Louis Art Museum) and the first, Museum of Modern Art version, of *Dance*. *Back II*, of 1913, and *Back III*, of 1916, were made contemporaneously with *Bathers by a River* (The Art Institute of Chicago). And *Back IV,* of c. 1931, dates to the period of Matisse's work on a mural on the theme of *Dance* for the Barnes Foundation. The sculptures cannot exactly be considered studies for these paintings, though. Rather, they clarified for Matisse his conception of the figure on a scale equivalent to that of the paintings he was preparing, and helped him to order his feelings about the figure when conceived at such a scale.

Back I was accompanied by a group of pen-and-ink drawings of a female model posed facing the wood-paneled wall of Matisse's studio (p. 56). But the absence of feet in the sculpture shows that the artist was thinking of a bather standing in a shallow pool. His 1909 painting *Bather* (p. 45) shows a similar figure, wading into the picture surface just as the figure in *Back I* appears to meld into the relief plane. Matisse forms an arabesque from the figure that winds through it from the relaxed right leg up to the bent left arm. Between these extremities, the line cuts deep into the spine, threatening dissection of the image into two parts, each an assembly of bulbous volumes.

The Back (II)
Nu de dos (II)

Issy-les-Moulineaux, spring–early autumn 1913
Bronze, 6' 2¼" × 47⅝" × 6" (188.5 × 121 × 15.2 cm)
Inscribed lower left: "Henri Matisse." Lower right:
"HM 2/10"
The Museum of Modern Art, New York.
Mrs. Simon Guggenheim Fund

Standing Woman Seen from Behind
Femme nue debout, de dos
[Study for "The Back (I)"]
[Étude pour "Nu de dos (I)"]

Issy-les-Moulineaux, [autumn 1909]
Pen and ink on paper, 10½ × 8⅝" (26.6 × 21.7 cm)
Signed lower right: "Henri-Matisse"
The Museum of Modern Art, New York.
Carol Buttenweiser Loeb Memorial Fund

Study for "The Back (II)"
Étude pour "Nu de dos (II)"

Issy-les-Moulineaux, [spring–early autumn 1913]
Pen and ink on paper, 7⅞ × 6¼" (20 × 15.7 cm)
Signed left of center: "H. Matisse"
The Museum of Modern Art, New York.
Gift of Pierre Matisse

The Back (III)
Nu de dos (III)

Issy-les-Moulineaux, [spring–summer 1916]
Bronze, 6' 2½" × 44" × 6" (189.2 × 111.8 × 15.2 cm)
Inscribed lower left: "Henri M." Lower right: "H.M 1/10"
Founder, C. Valsuani
The Museum of Modern Art, New York.
Mrs. Simon Guggenheim Fund

Four years later, in *Back II* (p. 57), part of the spinal crevice has been filled in, yet the cuts that remain have been deepened and extended. Matisse told his students to "feel a center line in the direction of the general movement of the body and build about that." He thus straightens the spine, aligns it with the inner contour of the left leg, and forms branches that divide up the blocked-in parcels of mass that surround it. A small study (p. 56) shows a reminder of the old, arabesque conception. That was almost entirely discarded to produce this Cubist giant, coarsely chiselled and abraded, slumbering against a wall.

With *Back III*, of 1916, an even more astonishing transformation occurs. The full extent of the spine has returned, but now in relief, utterly straightened, and attached to the head so that it reads as a fall of long hair. As in the case of *Bathers by a River*, the figure presents a series of bold, broad vertical zones of light and dark tonalities that fracture it into parts and yet recompose it in their repetitive rhythms. The vestigial sense of an arabesque in the preceding relief is replaced by the parallel uprights of trunklike legs, limp but weighty right arm, adjacent flattened area of back, and long fall of hair which functions as the fulcrum around which the other forms are balanced.

The Back (IV)
Nu de dos (IV)

Nice, place Charles-Félix, [c. 1931]
Bronze, 6' 2" × 44¼" × 6" (188 × 112.4 × 15.2 cm)
Not inscribed, not dated
Founder, C. Valsuani
The Museum of Modern Art, New York.
Mrs. Simon Guggenheim Fund

Although *Back IV*, made some fifteen years later, completes the process of simplification, it is no longer the product of explorative modeling, of a vigorous attack on the figure. It builds on those things, but its purity and utter tranquility are of an entirely different and far more distanced order.

This final relief comprises three simple vertical zones, much enlarged from before in relation to the ground, to whose rectangular shape they are locked by the newly prominent negative areas of the relief. The interaction of figure and ground is therefore much more a matter of design than it was in the previous states. Indeed, the nearly symmetrical harmony of the work, the homogeneous nature of the surface, and the fluidity of the contours, which creates one uninterrupted flow from top to bottom, all speak of Matisse's willingness to surrender the expressiveness of individual parts to that of the designed surface as a whole. This reflects his turn from the descriptive detail of the Nice period to the new simplicity of his work of the 1930s. "I nowadays want a certain formal perfection," he said in 1929, "and I work by concentrating my means. . . ." This sculpture remained in Matisse's studio to the end of his life, where its reductive purity, the outcome of a development going back to his earliest decorative paintings, was totally in harmony with his last decorative works, the large-scale cutouts, for whose simplified, separated forms this work prepared.

View of Collioure and the Sea
Vue de Collioure et la mer

Collioure, summer 1911
Oil on canvas, 23⅞ × 19⅝" (61 × 49.6 cm)
Signed lower left: "Henri-Matisse"
The Museum of Modern Art, New York.
Nelson A. Rockefeller Bequest
Formerly collection Michael and Sarah Stein

Matisse was "at the crossroads of modern painting" in 1911, Jack Flam has observed. When he painted *View of Collioure and the Sea* in the summer of that year, he was in some ways taking a look back. Returning to a motif he had first painted in 1905, he turned away from the synthetic, abstracted treatment that he had established in his art to a more conservatively empirical and analytical approach.

This landscape is not as casual a work as it first appears. Its soft brushwork and vivid color are controlled and counterpointed by the angular drawing that carries the eye up the surface, telescoping depth. Repetitions of similar forms in different spatial positions assist this effect. The pink-red rooftop in the valley points up to the complementary-colored roof of the church above; the tower of the church, arch of the bridge, and round blob of a tree in the foreground likewise help to draw together the three schematically divided zones of the painting in which these forms are located.

In an interview he gave that autumn, Matisse spoke of his utter pleasure in the Collioure landscape and of his belief that it was the most beautiful in the south. Every day, he said, he would take walks in the hills that skirt the coast, and on numerous occasions try to paint the landscape, only to find it impossible to reproduce its beauty. Since this was possibly one of only two Collioure landscapes he kept (and exhibited) from that summer, we may reasonably assume that in it he felt a rare satisfaction.

Still Life with Aubergines
Nature morte aux aubergines

[Collioure, summer 1911]
Oil on canvas, 45¾ × 35⅛" (116.2 × 89.2 cm)
Signed lower left: "Henri-Matisse"
The Museum of Modern Art, New York.
Gift of Mrs. Bertram Smith

Perhaps it was because Matisse found Collioure more beautiful a landscape than he could hope to re-create by painting it directly that his major effort, in the summer of 1911, turned toward transposing the effect of landscape to an interior setting, in the decorative *Interior with Aubergines* (at the Musée de Grenoble), for which this *Still Life with Aubergines* served as a study.

This still life is essentially a geometric composition of the three primary colors supported by their complementaries; its elements come together to form such an unconstrained whole largely because of Matisse's lively touch. Being so spontaneously and, more important, so lightly brushed, the ground is allowed to breathe and to show through, enlivening the brilliance of the color and giving a joyous sense of spaciousness and airiness to the work. When Jean Leymarie later told Matisse that according to an Oriental proverb to dream of three aubergines was a sign of happiness, Matisse was apparently delighted.

Depicted beside the aubergines, however, is a ten-inch-high plaster cast of a sixteenth-century Florentine *Ecorché* (or flayed figure), then believed to be a work by Michelangelo. The flayed man in Matisse's painting, dwarfed by a rounded voluptuous pot and isolated within a halo of flame-red brushstrokes from the exotically colored fruit, seems to connote the frailty of human presence, casting a note of unease in the paradisal garden represented in miniature by the profuse splendor of the still-life setting.

The Red Studio

L'atelier rouge [Le panneau rouge]

Issy-les-Moulineaux, [autumn 1911]
Oil on canvas, 71¼" × 7' 2¼" (181 × 219.1 cm)
Signed lower left: "Henri-Matisse"
The Museum of Modern Art, New York.
Mrs. Simon Guggenheim Fund
Formerly collection George Tennant

"You are looking for the red wall," Matisse said to a visitor who came to his studio shortly after this painting was completed; "this wall does not exist at all! . . . Where I got the color red—to be sure, I do not know. . . . I find that all these things, flowers, furniture, the chest of drawers, only become what they are to me when I see them together with the color red." Close inspection shows that the walls in *The Red Studio* were originally painted a blue-gray, and the furniture against the back wall a pale yellow ocher. The matte red that replaced these colors resulted in Matisse's boldest attack to date on traditional three-dimensional illusionism. It erases the division of floor and wall and the angle of the corner of the studio. There are no depicted volumes at all. Anything inherently three-dimensional becomes either a flattened plane or is reduced to a linear diagram through which the space of the room is allowed to pass. And yet, interiority is implied in the arrangement of objects and by the curtained window at the left, whose pale blue-green darkens the space of the studio—except for the glowing works of art that form a kind of Advent Calendar on the walls.

This exhibition of Matisse's art is dominated by compositions of figures in passive poses. And the empty chairs in front of them serve to remind us of Matisse's ideal of art as a rest from physical fatigue. Time is momentarily arrested; the face of the tall clock has no hands. Yet everything is immanent with movement. The works of art seem ready to keep circulating in space, and, in the foreground, the box of crayons suggests that the artist is about to continue his work.

Periwinkles/Moroccan Garden

Les pervenches/Jardin marocain

Tangier, winter–spring 1912
Oil, pencil, and charcoal on canvas, 46 × 32¼" (116.8 × 82.5 cm)
Signed and dated lower left: "Henri-Matisse-1912"
The Museum of Modern Art, New York.
Gift of Florene M. Schoenborn
Formerly collection Paul Guillaume

This painting, which takes its name from its scattered accents of pale blue periwinkles, was made during Matisse's first trip to Morocco. Although seemingly an extremely spontaneous work, its free handling in fact covers the most meticulously drawn layout in pencil, which Matisse followed very carefully indeed, hardly ever allowing his brushwork to cross predetermined lines. In establishing the design first, then coloring it afterwards, Matisse continues the approach of works like *The Red Studio* (p. 67). Only here, the coloring disguises the deliberated design process, giving the impression of a freely invented work.

"I found the landscapes of Morocco," Matisse said, "just as they had been described in the paintings of Delacroix and in Pierre Loti's novels." Matisse's own paintings made in Morocco are in turn familiar to us. This one, for example, contains an element of Art Nouveau decoration in its arabesque patterning and hot-house colors. It uses this decorativeness to distance the landscape from a specific location, thereby to idealize it. While in Morocco, Matisse read Dickens, the first writer to see the life of his times as a gigantic pulsation toward and away from the great industrial centers and to see these centers as spreading cancers on a green landscape. Matisse's painting is not only about Morocco, but also about what he left behind when he went there. The artist turns his back on the modern European city to imagine a utopia far away. Like Delacroix and Loti, though, he imagines it in a French colony; therefore, in a place still available to the government of his imagination when he returns home.

Goldfish and Sculpture
Poissons rouges et sculpture

Issy-les-Moulineaux, [spring–summer 1912]
Oil on canvas, 45¾ × 39½" (116.2 × 100.5 cm)
Signed lower left: "Henri Matisse"
The Museum of Modern Art, New York.
Gift of Mr. and Mrs. John Hay Whitney
Formerly collection Hans Purrmann

A figure in Matisse's arcadian composition of 1906, *Le bonheur de vivre*, was the original source for his sculpture represented in this painting of his studio. This representative of arcadia brings with her the sensual indolence of her original setting, which suffuses this simple interior with something of the same hedonistic spirit. Being also a work of art, the sculpture is representative, too, of contemplative meditation, as are the flowers and goldfish. All three elements of the still life—the woman, the flowers, and the goldfish—are no longer in their natural states, but are transformed or contained to serve a decorative purpose.

For Matisse and his contemporaries, goldfish signified the exotic and oriental. To place the goldfish and the sculpture each side of a vase of cut flowers was as if to bring together the exotic and the arcadian, and assert their common harmony. Ultimately, though, it is the harmony of art and nature—of making art from, and as one with, nature—that is the controlling metaphor of this work. This metaphor is also expressed by the spreading sea greens that spill out beyond the goldfish bowl to the dish below and open doorway above, as if the contents of the aquarium had soaked into the very fabric of the painting. And it is integral to the meaning of the blue field, which, seeming to dissolve the solidity of the objects within it, is an imagination of open air within the artist's studio.

The Blue Window

La fenêtre bleue [La glace sans tain]

Issy-les-Moulineaux, [summer 1913]
Oil on canvas, 51½ × 35⅝" (130.8 × 90.5 cm)
Signed lower left: "Henri-Matisse"
The Museum of Modern Art, New York.
Abby Aldrich Rockefeller Fund
Formerly collections Karl-Ernst Osthaus;
Museum Folkwang, Hagen and Essen

The Blue Window was painted in the Matisses' bedroom of their house at Issy-les-Moulineaux, before a window looking out over the garden, with its willow-pattern-like trees and huge spherical bushes, to the studio in the background, over which hovers a large oval halo of a cloud. On the table or shelf in front of the window we see a still life of domestic objects: the cast of an antique head, a vase of flowers set on a circular mat, a small decorated jar, a yellow-ocher dish containing a blue brooch, and what is probably a square mirror with a red frame. On the windowsill behind the mirror is a lamp, which had possibly been in Matisse's possession since his student days, and seemingly fastened to the wall at the left is a green Chinese vase. The painting is, as Alfred H. Barr, Jr., has written, "all verticals and horizontals, as structural as scaffolding, against which are hung the free forms of the still life and landscape. Each object is . . . isolated and simply rendered. . . ."

And yet, as Barr points out, the isolation of the objects "is subject to whimsical magic," which brings them together in unexpected and illogical ways, thus joining the space of the room to that of the garden outside. When asked why he was attracted to the motif of the window, Matisse replied: "for me space is one unity from the horizon right to the interior of my workroom . . . the wall with the window does not create two different worlds." All of his paintings of windows establish the contiguity of the outside space of nature and the man-made space of the interior.

Woman on a High Stool (Germaine Raynal)
Femme au tabouret (Germaine Raynal)

Paris, quai Saint-Michel, [early 1914]
Oil on canvas, 57⅞ × 37⅝" (147 × 95.5 cm)
Signed lower left: "Henri-Matisse"
The Museum of Modern Art, New York.
Gift of Florene M. Schoenborn and Samuel A. Marx

The subject of *Woman on a High Stool* is Germaine Raynal, the wife of the Cubist critic Maurice Raynal. Matisse's portrait is hardly guaranteed to please even so sophisticated a sitter. Her face is reduced to an oval mask, set on a straight neck whose parallel lines are repeated to articulate the torso as well. The figure has been described as gaunt and emaciated, conveying a sense of misery and mute endurance. It can, in fact, hardly be described as a portrait. The severe linear architecture and enveloping gray ground, both reminiscent of Analytical Cubist paintings, seem actually to be destroying the material substance of the sitter. The way that Matisse has carried the background into the seat of the stool causes the figure to seem levitated in front of the canvas surface, apparently suspended from a line created by the change of gray tones to the right of her head. This kind of painting into the contours was familiar to Matisse from the late work of Cézanne, and he used it often in this so-called experimental period of his art—though never again to quite such disturbing effect.

The sheet of paper shown on the back wall seems to hang down over the top of the canvas, and repeats its narrow vertical shape. It contains a painting of a vase by Matisse's then teen-age son, Pierre, which echoes the abstractness of the figure beside it in a deliberated formal analogy that seems almost humorous in this severe context. The *Woman on a High Stool* itself was to fulfill a rather similar function in the top right corner of the *Piano Lesson* (p. 89) two years later.

View of Notre-Dame

Une vue de Notre-Dame

Paris, quai Saint-Michel, [spring 1914]
Oil on canvas, 58 × 37⅛" (147.3 × 94.3 cm)
Signed lower left: "H Matisse"
The Museum of Modern Art, New York.
Acquired through the Lillie P. Bliss Bequest, and the Henry Ittleson, A. Conger Goodyear,
Mr. and Mrs. Sinclair Funds, and the Anna Erickson Levene Bequest given in memory of
her husband, Dr. Phoebus Aaron Theodor Levene

Although we know that this picture was painted from the window of Matisse's Paris studio at 19, quai Saint-Michel, looking down the Seine to the cathedral of Notre-Dame, its specific subject is hardly recognizable. The repoussoir window jamb, instead of offsetting an illusion of depth, becomes part of an insistent surface geometry of spontaneously drawn black lines that organizes the blue monochrome of the work, an "aerated" blue modified only by the patch of very light pink on the facade of the cathedral and the vivid green of the tree beside it.

Pentimenti visible beneath the blue surface suggest that the painting was originally sketched out in fairly close conformity to the motif. Indications of the balcony of the window, to the right, and of buildings and the far quai of the Seine, to the left, show what Matisse excised from the scene. The cathedral has clearly been enlarged and moved higher in the painting, the roof of the transept now carrying to the same height as the towers did originally. Even from the start, however, Matisse seems to have avoided showing anything of the Gothic character of Notre-Dame. It is a blocky Romanesque structure, except that it seems to have collapsed onto the picture plane.

Matisse had habitually been using large areas of open color, but never had he given a single, spontaneously painted field of color such command of a work as he does here—and it is this that makes it seem so radical. Perhaps Matisse himself found it too radical. It would not be exhibited until 1966, after his death. Immediately, its influence was felt on contemporary American painting.

Matthew Stewart Prichard

Paris, quai Saint-Michel, [summer 1914]
Etching, printed in black: composition 7⅛ × 4¾"
(18.1 × 12.1 cm); sheet 15¾ × 11¼" (40 × 28.5 cm)
Signed lower right of sheet in ink: "essai/
H. Matisse"
The Museum of Modern Art, New York.
Purchase Fund

Yvonne Landsberg

Paris, quai Saint-Michel, July 1914
Pen and ink on paper, 25⅝ × 19⅞" (65 × 50.2 cm)
Signed and dated lower right: "Henri-Matisse/
Juillet 1914"
The Museum of Modern Art, New York.
Alva Gimbel Fund

Charles Bourgeat (Resembling Dr. Vassaux)
Charles Bourgeat (ressemblant à Dr. Vassaux)

Paris, quai Saint-Michel, [1914]
Etching, printed in black: composition 7¹/₁₆ × 5⅛"
(18 × 13 cm); sheet 14¾ × 11" (37.5 × 28 cm)
Signed lower right of sheet in ink: "tirage à quinze
exempl./ troisième epr./ Henri-Matisse"
The Museum of Modern Art, New York.
Acquired through the Lillie P. Bliss Bequest

Mlle Yvonne Landsberg

Paris, quai Saint-Michel, [spring–summer 1914]
Etching, printed in black: composition 7⅞ × 4⁵/₁₆"
(20.1 × 11 cm); sheet 17¹¹/₁₆ × 12½" (45 × 31.8 cm)
Signed lower right of sheet in ink: "f. a-quinze ed/
quatrième ép./ Henri-Matisse-"
The Museum of Modern Art, New York.
Gift of Mr. and Mrs. E. Powis Jones

In the spring and early summer of 1914, Matisse painted perhaps the most extraordinary of his portraits affected by Cubism, that of Yvonne Landsberg, now in the Philadelphia Museum of Art. The subject of this dramatic and somewhat forbidding picture was, in fact, extremely shy and self-effacing. The Museum's drawing of Yvonne Landsberg, one of an extended series that accompanied, rather than served as studies for, the painting, conveys the timidity of the nineteen-year-old not only in the cautiousness of her gaze but also in the frailty Matisse has drawn into the posture with thin, wiry lines.

While waiting for his subject to arrive for the first sitting, Matisse spent the morning making drawings of magnolia buds which, he said, Yvonne Landsberg reminded him of. These buds, and their leaves, appear around the margins of the etching he made of her, and are repeated in other portrait etchings of the same period.

These small etchings were apparently made at astonishing speed after careful study of the sitter; a small hand-press was installed in his studio so that Matisse could quickly see the printed result. Utterly different from his severe paintings of the period, they serve as a reminder that even in this period of extreme abstraction, the record of observed reality continued to be important to the artist. They are also among the freshest, simplest, and most decisive of all his prints.

Goldfish and Palette
Poissons rouges et palette

Paris, quai Saint-Michel, autumn 1914
Oil on canvas, 57¾ × 44¼" (146.5 × 112.4 cm)
Signed lower right: "Henri-Matisse"
The Museum of Modern Art, New York.
Gift of Florene M. Schoenborn and Samuel A. Marx
Formerly collection Jacques Doucet

The most puzzling zone of this remarkable painting is that to the right. However, in a postcard to the painter Charles Camoin, Matisse explained that it contains "a person who has a palette in his hand and who is observing." The reverse of that postcard comprised a reproduction of Albrecht Dürer's famous print of *St. Jerome in His Study*, where the saint is writing beside tall vertical windows, with a band of shadow between them. There is something utterly ascetic about Matisse's work, too. It looks back to the subject of his *Goldfish and Sculpture* of 1912 (p. 71), yet the grace and lightness of the earlier work has turned into severity and barely relieved darkness.

Goldfish and Palette was painted in a period when Matisse was in close contact with Cubist artists, especially with Juan Gris, whose influence may be discovered in the triangulated, cage-like treatment of the upper right corner. Matisse's painting is anti-Cubist, however, in the sense of light it provides. The dark vertical band that connotes interior shadow is warmed by underpainting and by the soft mauves and greens of the partly scraped-over legs of the table on which the still life stands. The screening of the window created by this band traps space inside the room, and prevents the window from opening optimistically onto the outside world. Indeed, outside the limits of this band nearly everything is cold and severe. Within it, however, the rich orange-and-yellow fruit and especially the red-and-magenta goldfish radiate a brilliant light that seems to infuse the scumbled white of the tabletop and the milky water of the aquarium. In the first winter of the Great War, Matisse evokes nostalgic memory of earlier, more joyous versions of the same theme.

Still Life after Jan Davidsz. de Heem's "La desserte"
Nature morte d'après "La desserte" de Jan Davidsz. de Heem

Issy-les-Moulineaux, [summer–]autumn 1915
Oil on canvas, 71¼" × 7' 3" (180.9 × 220.8 cm)
Signed lower right: "Henri-Matisse"
The Museum of Modern Art, New York.
Gift of Florene M. Schoenborn and Samuel A. Marx
Formerly collection John Quinn

If any one painting by Matisse qualifies for the description "experimental," which is often applied to his entire work from 1914 through 1916, then this is surely it. Indeed, the artist himself spoke of having made it using "the methods of modern construction." By this, he meant the methods of Cubism. It is ironical, of course, that Matisse chose as his subject a famous seventeenth-century Dutch still life in the Louvre, which he had more faithfully copied when he was a student. His most "modern" painting is, thus, of a subject that is "ancient" both intrinsically and in the artist's own career. Presumably, the irony of this was not lost on Matisse himself, but, rather, contrived.

In one respect, then, the painting was a "sport," an anomalous experiment made to explore the potential usefulness of a new vocabulary without actually committing to it. Yet it was far more than that. Having allowed Cubism to infiltrate his art for some two years, he finally met the challenge head on in this large, ambitious, and programmatic work. Thus, it was a testing ground for a final understanding of what elements of Cubism might be harmoniously combined with his own practice.

Matisse would contrast the basis of Cubist art, in observed reality, with that of his own, in imagination, yet he insisted that "in those days we didn't feel imprisoned in uniforms, and a bit of boldness, found in a friend's picture, belonged to everybody." The military metaphor reminds us that "those days" were during World War I, and adds a further irony to this painting of worldly plenitude made mechanically austere in a period of anxiety and privation.

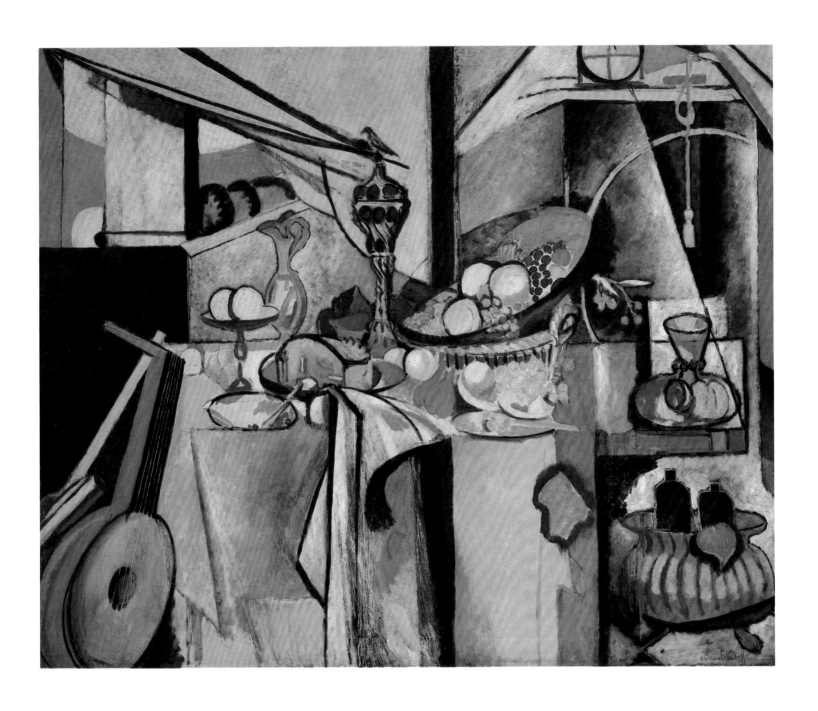

Half-length Nude
Nu à demi allongé

[Issy-les-Moulineaux or Paris, quai Saint-Michel, winter 1913–14]
Drypoint: composition 5¹¹⁄₁₆ × 3¹⁵⁄₁₆" (14.5 × 10 cm); sheet 12¹³⁄₁₆ × 9¹⁵⁄₁₆" (32.5 × 25.2 cm)
Signed lower right of sheet in ink: "Essai/ Henri-Matisse"
The Museum of Modern Art, New York. Purchase Fund

Three-quarter Nude, Head Partly Showing
Nu du trois-quarts, une partie de la tête coupée

[Issy-les-Moulineaux or Paris, quai Saint-Michel, winter 1913–14]
Transfer lithograph, printed in black: composition 19¾ × 12" (50.3 × 30.5 cm); sheet 19¾ × 12¹⁵⁄₁₆" (50.3 × 32.9 cm)
Signed lower left on the stone: "HM" and lower left in ink: "25/50"
The Museum of Modern Art, New York. Frank Crowninshield Fund

Seated Nude, Back Turned
Nu assis, vue de dos

[Issy-les-Moulineaux or Paris, quai Saint-Michel, winter 1913–14]
Lithograph, printed in black: composition 16⅝ × 10⅜" (42.3 × 26.4); sheet 19¹³⁄₁₆ × 13" (50.3 × 33 cm)
Signed lower right on the stone: "H.M." and lower right in ink: "37/50"
The Museum of Modern Art, New York. Gift of Mrs. John D. Rockefeller 3rd

Standing Nude, Arms Folded
Nu debout, les bras croisés

[Paris, quai Saint-Michel, 1915]
Monotype, printed in black: composition 6¹⁵⁄₁₆ × 5¹⁄₁₆" (17.6 × 12.8 cm); sheet: 14¾ × 11" (37.5 × 28 cm)
Signed lower right of sheet in ink: "monotype/ Henri-Matisse"
The Museum of Modern Art, New York. Frank Crowninshield Fund

The prints that Matisse made just before and during the period of World War I include not only small etched portraits (p. 79) but also studies of the female nude, among them etchings and drypoints, monotypes, and larger works in transfer lithography. Like the etched portraits, the nude studies are reminders of Matisse's continued interest in recording observed reality at a time when his paintings were often severely abstract. Unlike the portraits, however, they additionally remind us of the persistence of sensuousness within the severity of this period's work. And, for Matisse, where there is sensuousness there is also, usually, simplification. These works pick up the thread of his 1906 lithographs (p. 37) and spin it more finely and economically.

The monotype *Standing Nude, Arms Folded*, illustrated here, is a marvel of economy. A mere ten lines and four squiggles conjure up the figure. As Riva Castleman pointed out, the use of a single line to depict the inner and outer contours of the arm is perhaps the closest Matisse comes to the abstraction of his contemporaneous paintings. Although the lithographs are not so utterly simplified, by and large, they nevertheless represent a very high moment in his graphic *oeuvre*. Line drawn with a cursive surety is juxtaposed with detail of an extraordinary delicacy, and together these elements compose the pictorial rectangle, reaching out to and folding back from its perimeters, molding space and modeling the figure at the same time.

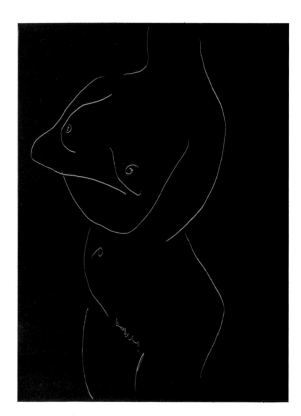

Gourds

Les coloquintes

Issy-les-Moulineaux, [late 1915–summer] 1916
Oil on canvas, 25⅝ × 31⅞" (65.1 × 80.9 cm)
Signed and dated lower left: "Henri-Matisse 1916"
The Museum of Modern Art, New York.
Mrs. Simon Guggenheim Fund
Formerly collections Léonide Massine; Paul Guillaume

Gourds is one of a group of still lifes of the mid-teens in which Matisse uses organic forms in a monumental fashion that is compatible with the severe, rectilinear geometry of his paintings of this period.

Matisse said of this work that it was "a composition of objects which do not touch—but which all the same participate in the same *intimité*," and that "in this work I began to use pure black as a color of light and not as a color of darkness." The relationship of the objects—which are isolated one from the next, but associated by virtue of the pressure of their surrounding ground—is crucial to the success of the painting, as Alfred Barr noted. "The background is a field divided diagonally into blue and black areas. Against this the objects neither stand nor hang—they simply exist. But they exist with the utmost clarity and vividness, their shapes vigorously drawn or modeled and silhouetted against the background like the isolated loaves and utensils strewn so carefully on the table of a Romanesque Last Supper."

Piano Lesson
La leçon de piano

Issy-les-Moulineaux, summer 1916
Oil on canvas, 8'½" × 6' 11¾" (245.1 × 212.7 cm)
Signed lower left of center: "Henri-Matisse"
The Museum of Modern Art, New York.
Mrs. Simon Guggenheim Fund
Formerly collections Paul Guillaume; Walter P. Chrysler, Jr.

The *Piano Lesson* is the most perfectly disciplined of Matisse's large-scale architectonic paintings of the mid-teens, and one of the most nearly abstract: the broad, open compartments of tranquil color that dominate the painting both flatten and enlarge the pictorial space and seem to have pushed out to the edges of the composition the few isolated images it contains. For all its formal clarity, however, this is one of Matisse's most elusive and ambiguous paintings, rich in his personal symbolism and full of subtle analogies and allusions.

The principal subject is Matisse's younger son, Pierre (then sixteen, but painted as a younger child), practicing on the Pleyel piano beside the open window of the family's living room. In the bottom left corner, we see a representation of one of Matisse's most sensual sculptures, the *Decorative Figure*, of 1908, and, diagonally opposite, one of his most severe paintings, *Woman on a High Stool (Germaine Raynal)*, of 1914 (p. 75). Their contrasted moods are echoed in another form by the objects on the piano top: a burning candle, traditionally symbolic of desire, and a metronome, standing for measure and order. The child must surely be seen as the father of the man, the artist who painted this picture, who therefore shows himself to be "such a romantic, but with a good half of the scientist, the rationalist," as he had described himself to a friend two years earlier.

Trapped in the geometry of the painting, the surrogate artist creates a visual music that scrolls over the music stand and into the arabesque grillwork below the green wedge of lawn.

The Rose Marble Table
La table de marbre rose

Issy-les-Moulineaux, [spring–summer 1917]
Oil on canvas, 57½ × 38¼" (146 × 97 cm)
Signed lower right: "Henri Matisse"
The Museum of Modern Art, New York.
Mrs. Simon Guggenheim Fund
Formerly collection Alphonse Kann

While many of Matisse's wartime canvases used muted tones, these tones were usually juxtaposed with brighter areas to create effects of dramatic contrast. The closely related pink and green on dark brown of *The Rose Marble Table*, although linked to a design of exceptional grandeur and formal clarity, eschews the dramatic to create a soft, lambent, and almost melancholy feeling that is all but unknown in Matisse's earlier work. Such a feeling may well have been evoked by the subject itself. Alfred Barr finds in the work a sense of "romantic gloom as if [it had been] painted at dusk." In any event, the impressive dignity of the painting owes much to the way in which Matisse joins so subtle and restrained a palette—which looks forward to his works of the Nice period—to a bold and reductive composition, typical of the period of structural experimentation now coming to a close.

It is one of Matisse's sparest and most open paintings. Although centralized in composition, it is centrifugal rather than centripetal in effect, for the eye is carried outward from the flat, tipped-up tabletop and across the relatively uninflected surround, which hardly reads as a ground, being in fact denser and more substantive than the image placed upon it. The effect is like that of a cutout. The shadowlike presences in the darkness, particularly the branches and foliage, at the top, and the garland of ivy, at the bottom, help to tie the image of the table to the perimeters of the work and serve to echo the forms of the open-lattice basket and the apples on the table itself. The entwining ivy and the trinity of fruit, two of Matisse's familiar emblems of the Golden Age, make the location into a paradisal garden, as well as the artist's own garden in the suburbs of Paris.

Interior with a Violin Case
Intérieur à la boîte à violon

Nice, Hôtel Méditerranée, winter 1918–19
Oil on canvas, 28¾ × 23⅝" (73 × 60 cm)
Signed lower right: "Henri-Matisse"
The Museum of Modern Art, New York.
Lillie P. Bliss Collection

Matisse himself described this painting as a "study of light—the sentimental association [created] out of the light of the interior and exterior." In May 1918, he had written to his friend Camoin of the beauty of the soft light of Nice, and, comparing Gauguin and Corot, he noted that the use of firmly drawn contours produced a "grand style" but the use of halftones was "much closer to the truth." At Nice, Matisse finally abandoned his own "grand style" in the search for greater truth. Had he continued with the former, he told an interviewer in June 1919, "I would have finally become a mannerist. One must always guard one's freshness, in looking and in emotion; one must follow one's instinct. Besides, I am finding a new synthesis. . . ." The style that Matisse was creating was no longer avant-garde. Yet in one basic respect, nothing had changed. He had always sought to create a harmony of light. Previously it had been produced by contrasts of color; now color was submitted to light itself.

More than twenty years later, Matisse still recalled with pleasure the almost theatrical opulence of the Hôtel Méditerranée, where this work was painted. Light came into the rooms "from below like footlights. Everything was fake, absurd, terrific, delicious. . . ." The room as painted here has indeed something of the sense of a stage set, but one from which all drama is deliberately excluded. As so often happens in Matisse's paintings of interiors, the artist himself is absent. Even his surrogate image, the violin, is missing from its sea-blue case, laid open upon the armchair in the foreground. But, then, the armchair is also a symbol of the restful and calming effects that Matisse hoped a painting like this would provide.

The Plumed Hat
Le chapeau à plumes

Nice, Hôtel Méditerranée, [winter–spring 1919]
Pencil on paper, 21¼ × 14⅜" (54 × 36.5 cm)
Signed lower right: "Henri Matisse"
The Museum of Modern Art, New York.
Gift of The Lauder Foundation, Inc.

This drawing belongs to a sequence of works, most in pencil, that comprise what is probably Matisse's most famous suite of drawings, as well as the first great achievement of his Nice period. The Plumed Hat series is named, of course, after the extraordinary hat worn by the nineteen-year-old model, who sat for the artist in 1919. This hat was Matisse's own creation of feathers and ribbon on a straw foundation, actually assembled on the model's head. "The plume is seen as an ornament, a decorative element," he told a visitor to his studio, "but it also a material; one can feel, so to speak, its lightness, and the down seems so soft, impalpable, one could very well be tempted to blow it away." The present drawing shows it with that kind of lightness, miraculously conjured at the center of some loose, fluffy lines.

Here, the model looks younger than her age, a girl dressing up as a woman. In this series, she is an actress. (Other drawings show her playing at being languorous, or seductive, or haughty, or demure.) And Matisse enjoys the artificiality of what he stages. For what distinguishes one part from the next is how he draws it. In this case, a certain lightness and transparency around the bodice, as compared to the heavier folds of the dress around the knees, evokes a note of coquettishness that attributes intention to the pose. The very carefulness of the drawing both eroticizes the young model for the artist and conveys a sense of protective vigilance on his part, the apparent uninterest of the sitter notwithstanding.

Young Girl Leaning by a Flowered Screen
Jeune fille accoudée au paravant fleuri

Nice, place Charles-Félix, [1923]
Transfer lithograph, printed in black:
composition 7¹/₁₆ × 10⁵/₁₆" (17.8 × 26 cm);
sheet 11⁷/₁₆ × 14¼" (29 × 36.2 cm)
Signed lower right of sheet in pencil:
"Henri-Matisse" and lower left of sheet in pencil: "47/60"
The Museum of Modern Art, New York.
Lillie P. Bliss Collection

Arabesque

Nice, place Charles-Félix, [1924]
Transfer lithograph, printed in black: composition
19¹/₁₆ × 12⁵/₈" (48.5 × 32.2 cm); sheet 24½ × 18⅛"
(62.2 × 46 cm)
Signed lower right of sheet in pencil: "Henri-
Matisse" and lower left of sheet in pencil: "5/50"
The Museum of Modern Art, New York.
Lillie P. Bliss Collection

Seated Nude with Arms Raised Before a Mantelpiece
Nu assis aux bras levés devant une cheminée

Nice, place Charles-Félix, [1925]
Transfer lithograph, printed in black: composition
25¹/₁₆ × 18¹³/₁₆" (63.6 × 47.8 cm); sheet: 29¹¹/₁₆ × 22¹/₁₆"
(75.5 × 56 cm)
Signed lower right of sheet in pencil: "3/50 Henri-
Matisse"
The Museum of Modern Art, New York.
Gift of Abby Aldrich Rockefeller (by exchange)

In the paintings that Matisse made in Nice in the 1920s, color was submitted to light: rather than producing light in the contrasts of color, as previously, his canvases were dosed with white, and the colors were joined and organized within this luminous substance. This was why lithography, which Matisse took up again in 1922 after eight years of almost complete absence from it, was especially attractive to him. It was particularly suited to an investigation of how tonal modeling could be reconciled with his longstanding concern for the decorative flatness of the picture surface. Before Nice, with the single exception of one 1906 lithograph (p. 37), all of Matisse's prints had been made exclusively from line. He would continue to make purely linear prints in the 1920s (p. 105), but tonally modeled works dominate his production in this decade.

These would eventually be of an extraordinary density, and no less amazing virtuosity (pp. 99, 107). At first, though, they are relatively light in tonality, and somewhat casual in feeling. The model, Henriette Darricarrère, is posed simply beside a vase of flowers that merges with the patterned wallpaper behind her, or she lounges in a floral costume that merges her with her similarly decorated armchair and background. By mid-decade, though, a new sense of monumentality is in evidence. These later lithographs, showing the same model, seated in the same armchair as the forementioned print but holding an extremely difficult pose, ultimately derive from drawings Matisse made from a cast of Michelangelo's *Night*. And they accompany the beginning of his most ambitious free-standing sculpture, *Large Seated Nude* (p. 101).

Large Odalisque with Bayadère Culottes
Grande odalisque à la culotte bayadère

Nice, place Charles-Félix, [1925]
Transfer lithograph, printed in black:
composition 21⁵⁄₁₆ × 17³⁄₈" (54.2 × 44.2 cm);
sheet 29½ × 22¹⁄₁₆" (75 × 56 cm)
Signed lower right of sheet in pencil: "15/50 Henri-Matisse"
The Museum of Modern Art, New York.
Nelson A. Rockefeller Bequest

By the mid 1920s, Matisse was using lithography to create an extraordinarily wide range of soft, closely graded tones—ranging from transparent, aerated grays to dense and sooty blacks—that appear to adhere to the surface of the sheet, and to release especially subtle effects of light from the luminous whiteness of the paper. What is more, the volumes thus created stayed "light" in feeling despite their solidity, and it was this "light," disembodied sense of volume that he sought in his contemporaneous paintings, too.

This highly finished lithograph is the last of a series of related works of 1924–25, which include *Seated Nude with Arms Raised Before a Mantelpiece* (p. 97), and it is surely among the masterpieces of Matisse's soft crayon style. The model, now relaxed in her pose and wearing striped culottes to make her into an "odalisque," is coiled in a chair with rich floral decorations that is boldly silhouetted against an indefinite dark ground. An analogy is clearly offered between woman and flower that, once grasped, asks us to read the torso of the model as if having emerged from the folded bud of her costume. Although at first glance a strikingly mimetic work, the print slowly puzzles in its lapses from resemblance: the absence of space for that part of the model's left arm that is not shown; the absence of the lower section of her right leg; the curious notation for her left foot. Two quite different orders of being appear to occupy the same figure, who will not look at us but is entirely self-absorbed and unexplaining. It is often said that Matisse's odalisques make up a fantasy. They do—but fantasy not in the sense of the incredible, not as something entirely separated from reality, but what reality can be confused with and mistaken for.

15/50 Henri-Matisse

Large Seated Nude
Grand nu assis

Nice, place Charles-Félix, [1925–29]
Bronze, 31¼ × 30½ × 13¾" (79.4 × 77.5 × 34.9 cm)
Inscribed: "HM 5/10"
The Museum of Modern Art, New York.
Gift of Mr. and Mrs. Walter Hochschild (by exchange)

This work, Matisse's largest fully three-dimensional sculpture, occupied him from 1925 through 1929 and marks, perhaps more than anything else he made, the shifting direction of his art in the second half of the 1920s. His so-called Nice period of that decade is often presented as if it were a single becalmed moment when Matisse relaxed into the arms of French tradition and constructed for himself a protected, domesticated arcadia, populated with odalisques in a colonialist imagination of a seraglio. This sculpture is chronologically and thematically continuous with images of odalisques (p. 99) and decoratively seductive nudes (p. 97), yet it transforms these images into a monumentality that we would do well to recognize, in some form, in its ancestors, too.

Quite soon after his arrival in Nice at the end of 1917, Matisse began to draw from a cast of Michelangelo's Medici Tomb *Night*, writing to a friend: "I try to assimilate the clear and complex conception of Michelangelo's construction." The pose of *Large Seated Nude*, and its ancestors, is generally indebted to the Michelangelo sculpture. It also refers to one of the *ignudi* on the Sistine Ceiling, which Matisse would have known. However, unlike these sources, and his own preceding prints as well, the figure is cantilevered in space, unsupported except by the mass of her abdominal muscles. We know from photographs of the work in progress that Matisse slowly increased it in size, elongated the torso, and lowered the angle of its elongation, thereby accentuating the outward thrust of the body into space. He also changed what had been a relatively smooth, rounded image into one with a broadly faceted surface, shaped by cuts of a knife into taut planes. The monumentality and gravity that was the result of these changes infused Matisse's paintings of the later 1920s as well.

Reclining Nude
Nu allongé

Nice, place Charles-Félix, [1927]
Pen and ink on paper, 10⅞ × 15" (27.7 × 32 cm)
Signed lower left: "H. Matisse"
The Museum of Modern Art, New York.
The Tisch Foundation, Inc. Fund

It is hardly surprising that line drawings such as this are central to Matisse's present reputation as a draftsman. It is decoratively beautiful and its beauty persuades us of a pleasurable naturalism even though it is far from that. Its conciseness, along with its beauty, argues a continuity with the classical drawing of the French past: since the early 1920s, comparison with Ingres had been a staple of Matisse criticism. But, unlike the more detailed of the 1920s drawings, it also seems fully continuous with the more radical elements of Matisse's art, an art of contouring, signs, and simplification.

Like Matisse's contemporaneous paintings, this drawing is an exercise in the assimilation of the figure into the decorated unity of the depicted interior, and of both into the unity of the surface conceived as a decoration itself. The model is formed in harmony with the contents of the studio, the patterned carpets and fabrics with arabesque ornamentation and latticework screens. And the drawing itself is a latticework, an all-over patterned fabric.

Yet the model, as Matisse would insist, is not just an "extra" in the interior. His models, he said, "are the principal theme of my work. . . ."

Odalisque with a Moorish Chair
Odalisque au fauteuil turc

Nice, place Charles-Félix, 1928
Pen and ink on paper, 25¾ × 19⅞" (65.4 × 50.5 cm)
Signed and dated lower right: "1928 Henri-Matisse"
The Museum of Modern Art, New York.
Acquired through the Lillie P. Bliss Bequest

Study of a Nude Seen Upside Down
Étude de nu renversé

Nice, place Charles-Félix, 1929
Etching, printed in black: composition 6⅝ × 9⁷⁄₁₆"
(16.8 × 24 cm); sheet 11¼ × 14¹⁵⁄₁₆" (28.5 × 38 cm)
Signed and dated lower right on the plate:
"1929 [backwards] Henri Matisse" and
lower right of sheet in pencil: "9/25/ Henri-Matisse"
The Museum of Modern Art, New York.
Gift of Mr. and Mrs. E. Powis Jones

Nude with a Moroccan Mirror
Nu au miroir marocain

Nice, place Charles-Félix, 1929
Etching, printed in black: composition 8⁹⁄₁₆ × 6"
(21.7 × 15.3 cm); sheet 14¾ × 11" (37.5 × 28 cm)
Signed and dated lower right on the plate: "29
[backwards] matisse" and lower right of sheet in
pencil: "12/25 Henri-Matisse"
The Museum of Modern Art, New York.
Gift of Mrs. Gertrud A. Mellon

In the second half of the 1920s, the odalisque became Matisse's principal vehicle for the representation of his models. He had seen women in seraglios when he visited Morocco in 1912 and 1913, and so, he said, "was able to put them in my pictures back in France without playing make-believe." Unquestionably, the memory of French colonial Africa lies behind the Nice odalisques. The drawing illustrated here shows a model in "oriental" costume lounging beside a Moorish chair.

Yet distant memories combine with present realities, and Matisse had to know that he was enrolling his models, and himself, in a masquerade. The game, nominally and partly about Africa, is also about something much closer at hand: the enclosed world of the Nice studio itself (filled with trappings such as the Moorish chair), its hermetic isolation from outside. The ideally separate world of Matisse's art found its appropriately separate location as if finding an appropriate style. And the way that the models are represented tells itself of isolation from outside. In the extraordinary small etchings, they dream beside goldfish bowls and the contours of their bodies glide into those of their surroundings. The surface of the paper divides into interlocking but mutually connected compartments that successively open and enclose form as if waves of movement were passing through the images drawn there. The ink, suspended on the surface by the nonabsorbent China paper, is thin and dry, and the lines it forms seem at once to meander and to be frozen in place. The self-sufficiency of these works is more than a purely formal one but tells of a world always imaginarily in movement but where nothing will ever change.

The White Fox
Le renard blanc

Nice, place Charles-Félix, [1929]
Lithograph, printed in black: composition 20¼ × 14½"
(51.4 × 36.8 cm); sheet 26⅟₁₆ × 19¾" (66.2 × 50.3 cm)
Signed lower right of sheet in pencil: "39/75/ Henri-Matisse"
The Museum of Modern Art, New York.
The Associates Fund

The title of this lithographic virtuosity refers, of course, to the fur worn by the model, which Matisse has rendered with obvious pride in his illusionistic powers. The model, owing presumably to her extraordinarily prominent, slanted eyes, was more frequently shown in the guise of an odalisque, and quite the most sensual of all the odalisques that he drew or painted. Some images of her are unashamedly erotic. The shock of the present work is increased if one knows these other images. But even without that knowledge, its swathing of sensuality in the trappings of bourgeois society remains a marvelously provocative conceit.

As with nearly all of Matisse's Nice-period images of women, this one is withdrawn into her own thoughts and feelings, with a self-absorption that—for all her allure—is protective of her. Here, the finery worn by the model is an additional armor as well as an invitation. And its invitation of tactile contact evaporates the more closely one approaches it, dissolving into the obsessively hatched lines of the crayon. As always, there are anomalies in the representation. The arm of the chair is a crude, hard presence that intrudes aggressively into the soft image. The part of the body that is beneath the fur is unimaginable from what Matisse has drawn, and the hand that dips beneath it blurs as it does so. We sense a bemused resignation in the model's face as well as in her posture, as if she is waiting for something, dressed up in this way. But that may be only from knowing the more usual, undressed images of this model, whose sensuality is simply immanent in this extremely complex work.

Venus in a Shell (I)
Vénus à la coquille (I)

Nice, place Charles-Félix, [late summer 1930 or 1931]
Bronze, 12¼ × 7¼ × 8⅛" (31 × 18.3 × 20.6 cm)
Inscribed: "2/10 HM"
The Museum of Modern Art, New York.
Gift of Pat and Charles Simon

Tiari
Le tiaré

Nice, place Charles-Félix, [late summer 1930 or 1931]
Bronze, 8 × 5½ × 5⅛" (20.3 × 14 × 13 cm)
Inscribed: "2/10/ HM."
The Museum of Modern Art, New York.
A. Conger Goodyear Fund

These two sculptures, made around the same time, both evoke places utterly distant from where Matisse made them, in Nice. One is a remembrance of Tahiti, which the artist had visited earlier in 1930; the other is symbolic of the mythological past. Yet while the summoning of distant places associates the sculptures with each other, the venues evoked are what principally account for the startling differences between them. One is smoothly stylized and almost biomorphic; the other, more firmly shaped and classical in its connotations. Matisse's habit of working in two modes at the same time could hardly have a more conspicuous demonstration.

The *Tiari* is at once an image of the eponymous flower (a species of gardenia), which Matisse remembered seeing a Tahitian woman wearing in her hair, and an image of the woman herself. The simplified oval of the head—which is also the center of the flower—with its pistil-like nose, is surrounded and surmounted by a group of petals or leaves—which are also bunches of hair—that grow from a smooth wedge of a stem fitted into the back of the smooth neck. The two stalks, human and botanical, combine to produce the same flower. It is an image unique in Matisse's sculpture for its punning ambiguity.

In contrast, *Venus in a Shell I* (Matisse would make a companion, more dissonant version in 1932) is derivative of the pose of his *Large Seated Nude* of 1925–29 (p. 101), only transformed to clarify its antique associations. Whereas the *Tiari* looks backwards biographically in Matisse's career, this sculpture looks forward to a renewed involvement with classical mythology that was beginning to make its mark on his illustrations for the poems of Mallarmé (p. 111), with some of which it shares an erect eroticism.

Poésies de Stéphane Mallarmé

Published Lausanne, Albert Skira & Cie,
October 1932; etchings composed Nice, place Charles-Félix,
and Paris, summer 1931–autumn 1932
Twenty-nine etchings, each page 13⅛ × 9⅞" (33.2 × 25.3 cm)
The Museum of Modern Art, New York.
The Louis E. Stern Collection

Le guignon *(Misfortune)*
La chevelure *(The Flowing Hair)*
Nymphe et faune *(Nymph and Faun)*

The *Poésies de Stéphane Mallarmé* was Matisse's first and, some would argue, his greatest illustrated book. Its twenty-nine etchings culminated an extended series of drawings and trial proofs that occupied the artist for well over a year, from the summer of 1931 through the fall of 1932. He was simultaneously working on his designs for the mural decoration for the Barnes Foundation. Both projects reintroduced into Matisse's art an iconography drawn from mythology that had been, with the rarest of exceptions, absent for some twenty years. With that iconography, there returned, too, the decorative simplicity of the earlier period, only now in an extraordinarily refined form.

In the Mallarmé book, the odalisques of the Nice period of the 1920s have been replaced by, or transformed into, nymphs who are ravished by satyrs or who sprawl and play in an arcadia. There are other subjects as well, including boats to travel to arcadia, and a great swan who lives there, all drawn in a line that is like a filament, a delicate thread on the paper. Matisse used, he said, "an even, very thin line, without hatching, so that the printed page is left almost as white as it was before printing." Perhaps he was thinking of Mallarmé's own assertion that "the intellectual core of the poem conceals itself, is present—is active—in the blank space that separates the stanzas and in the white of the paper: a pregnant silence, no less wonderful to compose than the lines themselves."

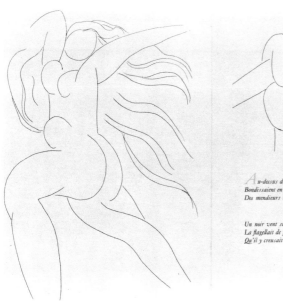

LE GUIGNON

*Au-dessus du bétail ahuri des humains
Bondissaient en clartés les sauvages crinières
Des mendieurs d'azur le pied dans nos chemins.*

*Un noir vent sur leur marche éployé pour bannières
La flagellait de froid tel jusque dans la chair,
Qu'il y creusait aussi d'irritables ornières.*

9

*Ses purs ongles très haut dédiant leur onyx,
L'Angoisse, ce minuit, soutient, lampadophore,
Maint rêve vespéral brûlé par le Phénix
Que ne recueille pas de cinéraire amphore*

*Sur les crédences, au salon vide : nul ptyx,
Aboli bibelot d'inanité sonore,
(Car le Maître est allé puiser des pleurs au Styx
Avec ce seul objet dont le Néant s'honore).*

*Mais proche la croisée au nord vacante, un or
Agonise selon peut-être le décor
Des licornes ruant du feu contre une nixe,*

*Elle, défunte nue en le miroir, encor
Que, dans l'oubli fermé par le cadre, se fixe
De scintillations sitôt le septuor.*

128

*Fausses entre elle-même & notre chant crédule ;
Et de faire, aussi haut que l'amour se module,
Évanouir du songe ordinaire de dos
Ou de flanc pur suivis avec mes regards clos,
Une sonore, vaine & monotone ligne.*

*Tâche donc, instrument des fuites, ô maligne
Syrinx, de refleurir aux lacs où tu m'attends !
Moi, de ma rumeur fier, je vais parler longtemps
Des déesses ; & par d'idolâtres peintures,
A leur ombre enlever encore des ceintures :
Ainsi, quand des raisins j'ai sucé la clarté,
Pour bannir un regret par ma feinte écarté,
Rieur, j'élève au ciel d'été la grappe vide
Et, soufflant dans ses peaux lumineuses, avide
D'ivresse, jusqu'au soir je regarde au travers.*

*O nymphes, regonflons des SOUVENIRS divers.
»Mon œil, trouant les joncs, dardait chaque encolure
»Immortelle, qui noie en l'onde sa brûlure
»Avec un cri de rage au ciel de la forêt ;
»Et le splendide bain de cheveux disparaît
»Dans les clartés et les frissons, ô pierreries !
»J'accours ; quand, à mes pieds, s'entrejoignent (meurtries*

80

Reclining Nude
Nu allongé

[Paris, boulevard du Montparnasse], July 1938
Charcoal on paper, 25⅝ × 31⅞" (60.5 × 81.3 cm)
Signed and dated lower right: "Henri Matisse 7/38"
The Museum of Modern Art, New York.
Purchase

Matisse tended to use softer, more pliable mediums—like pencil or charcoal—for explorative drawings. "A less rigorous medium than pure line," he wrote, ". . . enables me to consider simultaneously the character of the model, the human expression, the quality of surrounding light, atmosphere, and all that can only be expressed by drawing"—and from these things to condense the essential character in line. To wrest from the process of drawing linear images that signified not merely his models' appearance but "the emotional interest aroused in me by them" was the purpose of works such as this. Subsequently, he would make pen drawings—"no correction possible"—and there reimagine the purified images he had discovered. These finished products Matisse himself prized most. It is certainly arguable, however, that witnessing the struggle to achieve purification is more rewarding an experience than sight of the chaste result. The sublimity of Matisse's charcoal drawings, in which he searches and erases, and rubs down the forms, only to draw them again and again, tends certainly to support that proposition. In this audacious work, a true picture of creation and, superimposed, of its realization is revealed. "I am driven on by an idea," Matisse wrote, "which I really only grasp as it grows with the picture." We see in this drawing exactly what he means.

Matisse takes astonishing liberties with representation in order to channel and condense feeling in its linear armature. The emotional interest provoked in him by his models "does not appear particularly in the representation of their bodies, but often rather in the lines or the special values distributed over the whole canvas or paper, which form its complete orchestration, its architecture." Again, these are Matisse's words, to which he quickly adds, "It is perhaps sublimated sensual pleasure. . . ."

Branch of a Judas Tree
Branche d'un arbre de Judée

Nice-Cimiez, Hôtel Régina, August 1942
Charcoal on paper, 10⅜ × 15⅞" (26.3 × 40.3 cm)
Signed and dated lower right: "Henri Matisse 8/42"
Dedicated lower right, on June 17, 1952: "à John Rewald"
The Museum of Modern Art, New York.
Gift of John Rewald in memory of Frances Weitzenhoffer

This charcoal drawing generally relates to a vignette that Matisse designed for his illustrated book *Florilège des amours de Ronsard*, which would be published in 1948. Perhaps Matisse recalled this drawing, or one like it, when making the vignette. In any event, it belongs to an impressive sequence of plant drawings from the 1940s that also includes some of the famous Themes and Variations drawings, in which an explorative "theme" drawing in charcoal would be followed by "variations" in pencil or pen and ink. Viewed in this context, this present work should also be considered a theme drawing that aimed at discovering the essential structure of the motif.

In the same year that this drawing was made, Matisse had numerous extended conversations with his poet friend Louis Aragon that formed the basis of Aragon's introduction to the portfolio *Dessins: Thèmes et variations*, published the following year. Matisse spoke of drawing trees and their branches and leaves. "I shan't get free of my emotion," he said, "by copying the tree faithfully, or by drawing its leaves one by one *in the common language,* but only after identifying myself with it." To achieve this meant creating "signs." Referring to Claude Lorrain and Nicolas Poussin, he observed that "the way they place the sign that represents a leaf multiplies the leaves in the spectator's mind so that he sees two thousand of them." Then he added: "The importance of an artist is to be measured by the number of new signs he has introduced into the language of art. . . ."

This beautiful drawing was dedicated by Matisse to John Rewald, the great scholar of Impressionist and Post-Impressionist art who regularly visited the artist.

à John Rewald
Henri Matisse 8/42

Pasiphaé: Chant de Minos (Les Crétois)
by Henry de Montherlant

Published Paris, Martin Fabiani, 1944;
prints executed Nice-Cimiez, Hôtel Régina, and Vence, villa Le Rêve, 1943–May 1944
148 linoleum cuts: 18 full-page plates, cover, 45 decorative elements, 84 initials;
each page 12⅞ × 9¾" (32.7 × 24.8 cm)
The Museum of Modern Art, New York.
The Louis E. Stern Collection

> *". . . fraichie sur des lits de violettes . . . "*
> *". . . emportés jusqu'aux constellations . . . "*
> *". . . Mais soudain le soleil, secouant sa crinière . . . "*

Pasiphaé: Chant de Minos (Les Crétois), the second book that Matisse designed in its totality, uses linoleum engravings, which carried the images in relief and thereby allowed the simultaneous printing of text and plates. Matisse designed not only the full-page plates but also the decorative elements and cut initials, which are in red and serve to offset the balance of the light black-on-white text and the dark white-on-black plate on each spread. The artist added these initials, he said, because without them the work "seemed a bit funereal." Even more than with the Mallarmé book, the subjects of the plates mingle those that relate directly to the text with those, usually images of women, that do not, except in the most general way.

The compositional problem that faced Matisse was, like that of the Mallarmé book, of balancing a darker and a lighter page on a single spread, "except the two elements are reversed," he said. "How can I balance the black illustrating page against the comparatively white page of type? By composing with the arabesque of my drawing, but also by bringing the engraved page and the facing text page together so that they form a unit. Thus the engraved part and the printed part will strike the eye of the beholder at the same moment. A wide margin running all the way around both pages masses them together."

Matisse was particularly proud of his use of linoleum cuts. "I have often thought that this simple medium is comparable to the violin with its bow," he wrote. (He himself played the violin.) "The gouge, like the violin bow, is in direct rapport with the feelings of the engraver."

aintenant, toi, approche, fraîchie sur des lits de violettes.

Moi, le roi aux cils épais, qui rêve dans le désert ondulé,

moi, je vais rompre pour toi mon pacte fait avec les bêtes,

et avec les génies noires qui dorment la nuque dans la saignée

de mon bras, et qui dorment sans crainte que je les dévore.

Des sources qui naissent dans tes paumes je ne suis pas rassasié encore.

26

... fraîchie sur des lits de violettes...

Les oiseaux de l'extase ont leurs nids dans tes yeux.

La mélodie du monde inonde tes cheveux.

L'angoisse qui s'amasse en frappant sous ta gorge

crève contre ma bouche en un cri de bonheur.

Et moi, sans relâcher la bête que j'égorge,

j'adore sur ses traits cette chose qui meurt.

e l'ai frappée avec mes serres, et mes serres se sont teintées !

30

... emporté jusqu'aux constellations...

le délavement doux de nos brèves bontés,

comme on voit, quand l'aurore au ciel a éclaté,

des perles de rosée à l'airain de nos casques?

'ombre meurt. Le matin étonné se répand.

Que mon âme s'accorde avec le Tout-Puissant!

Prosterné sur le sol, je mâche la Matière.

Et, ma joue appuyée au sable frais, j'entends

42

... Mais soudain le soleil, secouant sa crinière...

Self-Portrait

Autoportrait

Vence, villa Le Rêve, or Paris, 1945
Crayon on paper, 16 × 20¾" (40.5 × 52.5 cm)
Signed and dated lower left: "45 HM"
The Museum of Modern Art, New York.
John S. Newberry Fund

Self-Portrait

Autoportrait

Vence, villa Le Rêve, June 1945
Pen and ink on paper, 20½ × 15¾" (52 × 40 cm)
Signed and dated lower left: "H Matisse 11 June 45"
The Museum of Modern Art, New York.
Gift of Philip Johnson (by exchange)

Matisse painted very few self-portraits; none after 1918. He made more paintings in which an artist, presumably him, appears in the company of a model or a still life, and yet more in which he appears in surrogate form. But self-portraiture, as such, is rare in his painting. It is more frequent in drawing, but even here it does not form any significant part of his art until after the mid-1930s, that is to say, until after he was in his mid-sixties.

These two drawings show Matisse a decade older than that. They were made in a period of extensive reexamination of the direction of his art, which seems to have provoked self-examination. Two years later, he would use a sequence of similar self-portrait drawings to illustrate a famous essay, "Exactitude is not truth," in which he defended himself against charges that his work was facile. His self-portraits, he said, seemed quite different yet clearly described the same man, "his character and his personality, his way of looking at things and his reaction to life." Matisse appears to have forgotten that the man he was referring to was himself, for with somewhat uncharacteristic candor he went on to describe "the reserve with which he faces [life] and which keeps him from an uncontrolled surrender to it," concluding: "It is indeed the same man, one who remains an attentive spectator of life and of himself."

These two drawings show this attentive spectator: in the act of self-representation and contemplating his self-representation as if in a mirror.

***Jazz* by Henri Matisse**
"Jazz" par Henri Matisse

Published Paris, E. Tériade, 1947, in an edition of 270 copies
Twenty pochoir plates plus text, each double sheet 16⅝ × 25⅝" (42.2 × 65.1 cm)
The Museum of Modern Art, New York.
The Louis E. Stern Collection

Matisse's most famous illustrated book, *Jazz*, was published in 1947 on the basis of paper cutout maquettes that he made in 1943 and 1944, to which he subsequently added a discursive text in his own bold handwriting. The cutouts were "reproduced" by using the same Linel gouache paints that colored them; their uneven coverage was retained by painting through stencils. Although Matisse was at first extremely disappointed with the result, as compared to the original cutouts, he was eventually encouraged by the tremendous reception his book received, particularly among painters. Its reputation continued to grow, and it is widely considered both a landmark in the history of printmaking and highly influential on subsequent "hard-edge" painting. As for Matisse himself, with this work, paper cutouts became central to his artistic practice and would increasingly occupy him, eventually to the exclusion of painting, in the last years of his career. Moreover, the juxtaposition of vividly colored cutout designs, for the plates of *Jazz*, and flowing black line, for its text, would soon after its publication form the basis of his decorations for the chapel he designed in Vence.

The imagery of *Jazz* evolved from many earlier works by Matisse, but its references to popular culture, reinforced by its very title, are new. The role of the text, Matisse wrote, was purely visual. Yet it comprises a series of very personal reflections on subjects ranging from airplanes to the artist's belief in God. Much in it stresses joy and happiness, yet there is a somber undercurrent to it, and to some of the plates. It was, after all, published shortly after the end of World War II, which fact adds poignancy to such images as that of the fall of Icarus, surrounded, it seems, by either stars or bursts of artillery fire.

The Clown *(Le clown). Plate I (frontispiece), with title page, from* **Jazz**

The Codomas *(Les codomas). Plate XI from* **Jazz**

Destiny *(Le destin). Plate XVI from* **Jazz**

The Knife Thrower *(Le lanceur de couteaux). Plate XV from* **Jazz**

un moment
si libres.
Ne devrait-on
pas faire ac-
complir un
grand voyage
en avion aux
jeunes gens
ayant terminé
leurs études.

54

Icarus *(Icare). Plate VIII from* **Jazz**

Circus *(Le cirque). Plate II from* **Jazz**

Dahlias and Pomegranates

Dahlias et grenades

Vence, villa Le Rêve, [spring–winter] 1947
Brush and ink on paper, 30⅛ × 22¼" (76.4 × 56.5 cm)
Signed and dated lower left: "H. Matisse/47"
The Museum of Modern Art, New York.
Abby Aldrich Rockefeller Fund

By the late 1940s, Matisse's artistic activity was divided between two mediums: large brush-and-ink drawings and paper cutouts. He envisaged the scheme of the chapel he designed at Vence as a chance to combine them, developing the ceramic-tile murals from drawings and the windows and chasubles from cutouts. And yet, in a sense, the two mediums were already connected, not divided at all.

Paper cutouts offered Matisse a way of drawing in color. The same may be said of *Dahlias and Pomegranates*. It offers no sense of outlines that have been filled in. The broad marks of the brush are planes as well as contours, and their own outlines have been generated, as it were, from the inside. Just as an outline in a cutout is inseparable from what is inside it, so it is here.

This drawing is also "colored" in the sense that the bold areas of ink modulate the sheet as a composition of compartmentalized white areas whose whiteness varies in color according to their size and to the varying pressures of the adjacent zones of black. The effect of vibration, and reciprocation, between positive and negative shapes recalls Matisse's Fauve woodcuts of 1906 (p. 37), only in more simplified form and more expansive format. Works such as this rival the paintings of the period in size, scale, and visual power. Indeed, Matisse effectively thought of such works as colored paintings in black and white.

The Necklace
Le collier

Nice-Cimiez, Hôtel Régina, May 1950
Brush and ink on paper, 20⅞ × 16⅛" (52.8 × 40.7 cm)
Signed and dated lower left: "H. Matisse/ Mai 50"
The Museum of Modern Art, New York.
The Joan and Lester Avnet Collection

The Necklace, drawn when Matisse was eighty, belongs to a sequence of nudes and mask-like faces in brush and ink (as here) or aquatint that bring to a great climax of simplification the style of drawing that he had invented in his Fauve woodcuts and lithographs of 1906 (p. 37).

Comparison to the woodcuts shows a similar sense of the sheet having been organized into compartments that carry different coloristic values in their whiteness according to the size of the areas that they occupy. Comparison to the lithographs shows a similar fluidity of line as it bends around the figural contours. By now, however, forty-four years later, the result is far more sophisticated, and deceptively simple. Even the two roughly parallel curves that stand for the lower part of the body compartmentalize the sheet, record the movement of the artist's hand, and provide a full sense of the volume of the body, all at the same time.

It is usual to stress the abstractness of such drawings. Yet the model seems credibly human, conjured up by some two dozen strokes of the brush, and another dozen jabs for the necklace. (One further jab that stood for the navel Matisse whited out.) Below the somewhat dour, bored face, the passage where the fingers play with the beads is of an astonishing descriptive virtuosity.

White Mask on Black Background
Masque blanc sur fond noir

[Nice-Cimiez, Hôtel Régina, 1949–50]
Aquatint, printed in black: composition 12½ × 9¹³/₁₆"
(31.8 × 24.9 cm); sheet 21¹¹/₁₆ × 14¹⁵/₁₆" (55.1 × 37.9 cm)
Stamped lower right of sheet: "HM."
The Museum of Modern Art, New York.
Purchased with funds given by Harry Kahn, Susan and
Arthur L. Fleischer, Jr., Carol and Bert Freidus,
Johanna and Leslie J. Garfield, Linda and Bill Goldstein,
Francine E. Lembo, Barbara and Max Pine, and
Susan and Peter A. Ralston in honor of Riva Castleman

This extraordinary image belongs to, but is unique in, a series of simplified aquatint heads that Matisse made in the late 1940s. It is the final image in the series, the rest of which comprise linear brush drawings printed in black on otherwise untouched white paper. This harsh, chalk-white face, a moon against the surrounding darkness, and its almost brutally marked features, could not afford a greater contrast to the images of ovals and arabesques that precede it.

Its title associates it with two paper cutouts of early 1950, *Negro Mask* and *The Japanese Mask* (both in private collections), although those are more abstracted works. The composition of the facial features here is reminiscent of that in a third paper cutout, a maquette (now apparently lost) for the poster of Matisse's exhibition of 1950 at the Maison de la Pensée Française, in Paris, where the famous *Luxe, calme et volupté* (Musée d'Orsay, Paris) was shown publicly for the first time since 1905. The poster design and this print bear a relationship to a group of lithographic illustrations of Eskimos that Matisse made in 1949.

All of these related works strongly argue an ethnographic association for this aquatint, and even an arcadian one, for the geographically and the mythologically distant were often companions in Matisse's work. Only, luxury, calm, and voluptuousness have been replaced here by something more primal and disturbing. Using charcoal attached to the end of a long cane, Matisse would draw faces similar to this on the ceiling of his bedroom in the last days of his life.

Maquette for cover of exhibition catalogue *Henri Matisse*

(New York, The Museum of Modern Art, 1951)
Paris, boulevard du Montparnasse, September 1951
Gouache on paper, cut and pasted, 10⅝ × 15¾" (27 × 40 cm)
Signed lower right: "HM"
The Museum of Modern Art, New York.
Commissioned by the Museum

Maquette for cover of *Matisse: His Art and His Public*, **by Alfred H. Barr, Jr.**

(New York, The Museum of Modern Art, 1951)
Paris, boulevard du Montparnasse, late summer 1951
Gouache on paper, cut and pasted, 10⅝ × 16⅞" (27 × 42.9 cm)
Signed lower left: "H.M." and lower right, across front: "H. Matisse"
The Museum of Modern Art, New York.
Commissioned by the Museum

These two cutout designs were commissioned from Matisse by The Museum of Modern Art in 1951: the first for the dust jacket of Alfred Barr's book *Matisse: His Art and His Public*, published that year; the second for the cover of the catalogue for the Museum's Matisse exhibition, also of 1951.

In making the design for the Barr book, Matisse seems to have thought, mistakenly, that he was being asked to design the book's binding rather than jacket. This would account for its relationship to patterns used in contemporaneous French art bookbinding, and for its somewhat muted coloration. When Matisse turned to the exhibition catalogue cover, he more than compensated in the freedom of both layout and color. With respect to the latter, he had been asked to restrict himself to three colors, to be printed on white, but found it impossible and unilaterally decided to use six colors plus white. With the agreement of the artist's estate, this cover design was reused for the catalogue of the Museum's 1992 exhibition *Henri Matisse: A Retrospective*.

Both designs are somewhat faded, owing to the fugitive nature of some of the gouache pigments that Matisse used. Thus, the latter in particular no longer fully possesses the vibrancy of coloristic relationships it originally had.

Maquette for red chasuble (front) designed for the
Chapel of the Rosary of the Dominican Nuns of Vence

Nice-Cimiez, Hôtel Régina, [late 1950–1952]
Gouache on paper, cut and pasted, 52½" × 6' 6⅛" (133.3 × 198.4 cm)
Not signed, not dated
The Museum of Modern Art, New York.
Acquired through the Lillie P. Bliss Bequest

Maquette for red chasuble (back) designed for the
Chapel of the Rosary of the Dominican Nuns of Vence

Nice-Cimiez, Hôtel Régina, [late 1950–1952]
Gouache on paper, cut and pasted, 50½" × 6' 6½" (128.2 × 199.4 cm)
Not signed, not dated
The Museum of Modern Art, New York.
Acquired through the Lillie P. Bliss Bequest

"In 1952, when I last saw Matisse in his studio at Nice," wrote Alfred Barr shortly after Matisse's death, "there were a score of the chasuble designs spread out on the walls like gigantic butterflies (p. 17). I could easily understand Picasso's enthusiasm for them. They seemed to me among the purest and most radiant of all Matisse's works." These chasubles were the last items that Matisse designed for the Chapel of the Rosary of the Dominican Nuns at Vence, close to his villa, Le Rêve, where he lived from 1943 to 1949.

The paper cutout was a particularly appropriate medium for creating the symbolic imagery that the chasubles required, since Matisse had developed this technique as a way of best producing what he called "signs" that condensed the essential characters of things. He had long felt that if the sign were to seem whole, color must not "simply 'clothe' the form: it must constitute it." This was achieved by "drawing with scissors on sheets of paper colored in advance, one movement linking line with color, contour with surface." "The cut-out paper," Matisse said, "allows me to draw in color. It is a simplification. Instead of drawing an outline and filling in the color—in which case one modified the other—I am drawing directly in color, which will be the more measured as it will not be transposed. This simplification ensures an accuracy in the union of the two means."

Although Matisse exercised great freedom in the design of the Vence chasubles, he nevertheless sought advice about the iconography appropriate to the festivals and periods of the Church calendar when each of the chasubles would be used. Additionally, the chasubles were made in the six prescribed liturgical colors—white, green, violet, red, rose, and black.

Each side of the red chasuble, reserved for the feasts of Pentecost and Martyrs, employs a central motif—a cross and a tree—surrounded by overlapping subordinate elements that symbolically connect the sacrifice of martyrs to the sacrifice of Christ. The green chasuble (p. 137), used from Christmas to Lent, and from Easter to Advent, connotes the hope of springtime in its color. The three palms or flames below the cross on the front symbolize the three theological virtues, Faith, Hope, and Charity; the five on the back are references to the five wounds of Christ. The black chasuble (p. 135), used for masses of the Dead, All-Souls Day, and Good Friday, carries on the front the word "Esperlucat," a colloquial Provençal term, meaning "to open one's eyes," and on the back a phoenix, symbol of promised resurrection. The white chasuble (p. 136), used on the feasts of Christ, the Blessed Virgin, and all nonmartyr saints, and on festive occasions, shows a plant-like form on the front, evocative of Christ's self-identification as the vine, while the tree-like motif of the back is an additional reference to Christ as the Tree of Life.

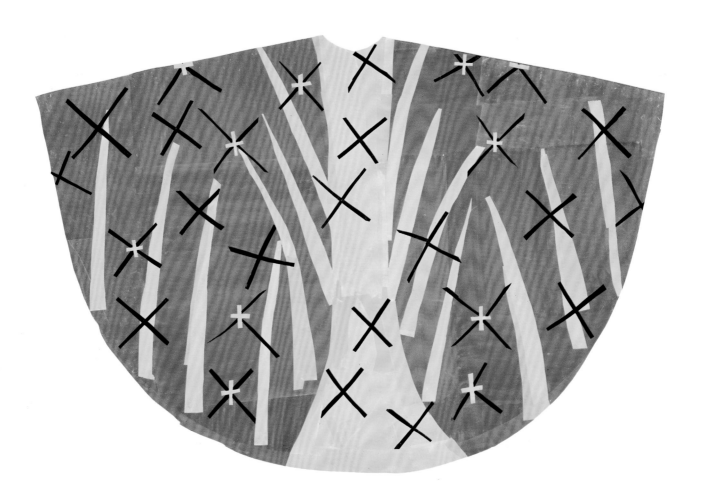

Black chasuble
La chasuble noire

Designed Nice-Cimiez, Hôtel Régina, [late 1950–1952]; executed 1955
Black crepe with white crepe appliqué, front: 47¾" × 6'4" (121.3 × 193 cm);
back: 48" × 6' 4" (121.9 × 193 cm)
Manufactured by Atelier d'Arts Appliqués, Cannes, France
The Museum of Modern Art, New York.
Gift of Philip C. Johnson

White chasuble
La chasuble blanche

Designed Nice-Cimiez, Hôtel Régina, [late 1950–1951]; executed 1951
White silk with yellow and green silk appliqué
front: 49" × 6' 6½" (124.4 × 199.4 cm); back: 50" × 6' 6½" (127 × 199.4 cm)
Manufactured by Atelier d'Arts Appliqués, Cannes, France,
Craftsman, Gustav Pederson
The Museum of Modern Art, New York.
Acquired through the Lillie P. Bliss Bequest

Green chasuble
La chasuble verte

Designed Nice-Cimiez, Hôtel Régina, [late 1950–1952]; executed 1955
Green silk (now faded to yellow) with black velvet, white and yellow silk appliqué,
front: 50¼" × 6'¼" (127.7 × 187.4 cm); back: 50⅛" × 6'¼" (127.4 × 187.4 cm)
Manufactured by Atelier d'Arts Appliqués, Cannes, France
The Museum of Modern Art, New York.
Gift of William Griffin in memory of his wife

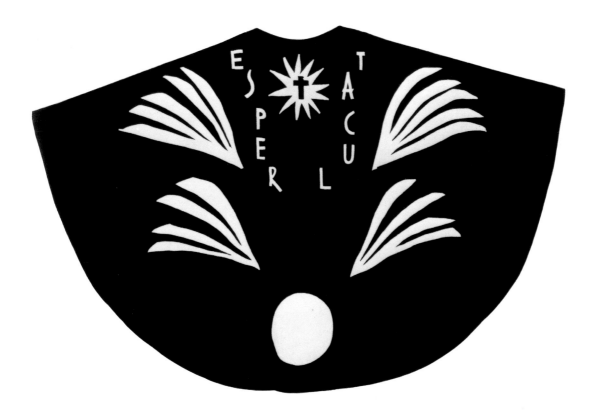

Black chasuble *(front)*

Black chasuble *(back)*

White chasuble *(front)*

White chasuble *(back)*

Green chasuble *(front)*

Green chasuble *(back)*

The Swimming Pool
La piscine

Nice-Cimiez, Hôtel Régina, [late summer 1952]
Nine-panel mural in two parts: gouache on paper, cut and pasted,
on white painted paper mounted on burlap; a–e, 7' 6⅝" × 27' 9½"
(230.1 × 847.8 cm); f–i, 7' 6⅝" × 26' 1½" (230.1 × 796.1 cm)
Not signed, not dated
The Museum of Modern Art, New York.
Mrs. Bernard F. Gimbel Fund

The Swimming Pool is by far the largest of Matisse's cutouts, with a total length just short of fifty-four feet. It is also his most ambitious. Its importance to Matisse is demonstrated by the fact that it was not produced in response to a specific commission, as were nearly all of his mural-size cutouts, but was made for himself, as an independent pictorial work to decorate the walls of his dining room at the Hôtel Régina, in Nice. Confined either to his bed or to a wheelchair, Matisse covered the walls of his apartment with groups of cutouts that together created the atmosphere of an idealized and lyrical natural world brought indoors. This environmental impulse was the motivating force of *The Swimming Pool.* "I have always adored the sea," he said, "and now that I can no longer go for a swim, I have surrounded myself with it."

"Shouldn't a painting based on the arabesque be placed on the wall, without a frame?" André Verdet had asked Matisse when discussing earlier cutouts. "The arabesque is only effective," Matisse replied, "when contained by the four sides of the picture." But he added a rider: "When the four sides are part of the music, the work can be placed on the wall without a frame." Here, the sides of frieze are, indeed, part of the music; the bathers leap in and out of the long rectangular strip, its taut whiteness stretched out like an elastic band. Its narrowness, whiteness, and geometry serve to accentuate the energy, rising at times to abandon, of the freely contoured blue forms that swim in the ideal aquatic world of Matisse's imagination.

LEFT: The Swimming Pool, *surrounded by brush-and-ink drawings, in the dining room of Matisse's apartment in the Hôtel Régina, Nice-Cimiez, c. 1952.*

BELOW: The Swimming Pool *(with* Women with Monkeys *above door) in the dining room of Matisse's apartment in the Hôtel Régina, Nice-Cimiez, c. 1952.*

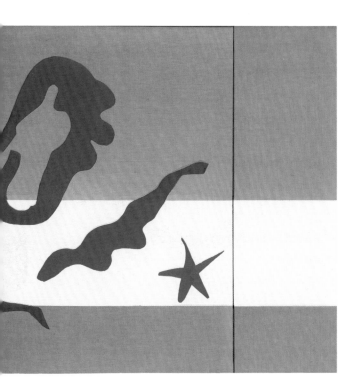

Christmas Eve
Nuit de Noël

Stained-glass window commissioned by Life *magazine, 1952*
Designed Nice-Cimiez, Hôtel Régina, early 1952; fabricated in the
workshop of Paul and Adeline Bony, Paris, [summer–autumn] 1952
Metal framework: 10' 11" × 54¾" × ⅜" (332.5 × 139 × 1 cm)
Signed lower pane of glass, lower right: "Matisse 52"
The Museum of Modern Art, New York.
Gift of Time, Inc.

Having enjoyed making the windows for the Vence chapel, Matisse became particularly attracted to using cutouts to design for stained glass. On January 15, 1952, after preliminary negotiations, he formally accepted a commission from *Life* magazine to design a stained-glass window on the general subject of Christmas.

Owing to the large size of the work—more than ten feet high—he used assistants to help him position, on the walls of his bedroom, the individual motifs he cut from pre-painted paper. The theme of the work became a starry Christmas Eve sky over a landscape of leafy organic forms with wave-like motifs at the bottom. But the three zones—sky, earth, and sea—intersect because Matisse carried the blue of the sky right down the center, where it surrounds a large, yellow algae form that balances the large, yellow star at the top. This strengthens the force of the symbolism as we read down the strata from blue sky to green and yellow earth to wine-dark sea.

The window itself was fabricated by Paul Bony, the stained-glass craftsman who had made the Vence chapel windows. On December 8, 1952, it arrived in New York and was displayed in the reception center of the Time-Life Building at Rockefeller Center in time for Christmas Eve. "If you have a chance to see it," Matisse wrote to Alfred Barr, "you will agree with me that a maquette for a stained-glass window and the window itself are like a musical score and its performance by an orchestra."

143

BIBLIOGRAPHICAL NOTE

The text of the present volume derives from two principal sources. The commentaries are, in the main, abridgements of those in the author's *Matisse in the Collection of The Museum of Modern Art* (New York: The Museum of Modern Art, 1978), to which the reader is referred for sources of quotations given here. That publication, given its antiquity, no longer reflects fully accurately either the composition of the Museum's collection or its author's understanding of the works in it. It is also needful of revision in some of its factual details. These have been checked against the research undertaken, under the supervision of Beatrice Kernan, for *Henri Matisse: A Retrospective* (New York: The Museum of Modern Art, 1992), from which the captions given here derive. My introduction to this present volume is an abridgement and revision of my section introductions in that publication.

The reader is referred to the bibliographical note in that publication for a summary of the enormous literature on Matisse; it would be redundant to reprint it here. Yet a few, essential volumes deserve mention again.

There are two invaluable collections of Matisse's writings: in French, Dominique Fourcade, ed., *Henri Matisse. Écrits et propos sur l'art* (Paris: Hermann, 1972); in English, Jack Flam, ed., *Matisse on Art* (London: Phaidon, 1973; revised edition, Berkeley and Los Angeles: University of California Press, 1995). The standard monograph, though now an historical monument and not entirely reliable in detail, remains Alfred H. Barr, Jr., *Matisse: His Art and His Public* (New York: The Museum of Modern Art, 1951). Louis Aragon, *Henri Matisse: Roman*, 2 volumes (Paris: Gallimard, 1971), translated as *Henri Matisse: A Novel* (London: Collins, 1972), comprises this poet's collected writings on Matisse, many of which the artist himself annotated. Pierre Schneider, *Matisse* (Paris: Flammarion, 1984; English edition, New York: Rizzoli, 1984) is a large and impressive volume with a rich, thematically organized text. Jack Flam, *Matisse: The Man and His Art*, 1869–1918 (Ithaca and London: Cornell University Press, 1986) is the best art-historical study in recent years. The same author's *Matisse: A Retrospective* (New York: Levin, 1988) is an extremely useful compilation of excerpts from critical writings on the artist from 1896 to 1957. Lawrence Gowing, *Matisse* (New York and Toronto: Oxford University Press, 1979) is an unsurpassed concise account of the artist's work.

J.E.

ACKNOWLEDGMENTS

In addition to those individuals mentioned on pages 7 and 9, we are grateful for the crucial participation of many additional staff members of The Museum of Modern Art and the High Museum of Art.

At The Museum of Modern Art we are grateful to Diane Farynyk, Registrar, and Lucille Stiger, Assistant Registrar, who oversaw the logistical details involved in transporting the exhibition to Atlanta. Important contributions were also made by Jerome Neuner, Director of Exhibition Design and Production, James Coddington, Chief Conservator, and Karl Buchberg, Conservator. The realization of this publication depended upon the skill and dedication of Lucy Adelman O'Brien, its editor, Emily Waters, its designer, Harriet Schoenholz Bee, the Museum's Managing Editor, Amanda W. Freymann, Production Manager, and Marc Sapir, Assistant Production Manager. Sharon Dec, Mr. Elderfield's assistant, and Mary Chan, Curatorial Assistant, provided invaluable support throughout all phases of the project.

At the High Museum of Art we are grateful to Marjorie Harvey, Manager of Exhibitions and Design, and Jody Cohen, Associate Registrar, who coordinated the complex logistics of mounting the exhibition in Atlanta. Susan Brown, Manager of Corporate Support, Keira Ellis, Manager of Foundation and Government Support, and Betsy Hamilton, former Manager of Individual Support, secured the financial support that made this exhibition possible. The efforts of Ann Hume Wilson, Manager of Public Relations and Marketing, and Roanne Katcher, Manager of Membership, were also critical to this project. Karen Luik, Eleanor McDonald Storza Chair of Education, oversaw development of the educational programming that accompanies the exhibition. Guidance in realizing this catalogue and all other exhibition-related publications was provided by Kelly Morris, Manager of Publications. Linda Boyte, Exhibitions and Design Assistant, Denise Kitchel, Assistant to the Deputy Director and Chief Curator, and Melissa Thurmond, Curatorial Assistant for Modern and Contemporary Art, provided essential assistance in all aspects of this endeavor.

PHOTOGRAPH CREDITS

INDEX OF ILLUSTRATIONS